CONSCIOUS BEING

AWAKENING TO YOUR TRUE NATURE

TJ WOODWARD

BALBOA.
PRESS

A DIVISION OF HAY HOUSE

Balboa Press books may be ordered through booksellers or by contacting:

Balboa Press
A Division of Hay House
1663 Liberty Drive
Bloomington, IN 47403
www.balboapress.com
1 (877) 407-4847

Because of the dynamic nature of the Internet, any web addresses or links contained in this book may have changed since publication and may no longer be valid. The views expressed in this work are solely those of the author and do not necessarily reflect the views of the publisher, and the publisher hereby disclaims any responsibility for them.

The author of this book does not dispense medical advice or prescribe the use of any technique as a form of treatment for physical, emotional, or medical problems without the advice of a physician, either directly or indirectly. The intent of the author is only to offer information of a general nature to help you in your quest for emotional and spiritual well-being. In the event you use any of the information in this book for yourself, which is your constitutional right, the author and the publisher assume no responsibility for your actions.

Any people depicted in stock imagery provided by Thinkstock are models, and such images are being used for illustrative purposes only.
Certain stock imagery © Thinkstock.

Print information available on the last page.

ISBN: 978-1-5043-2929-3 (sc)
ISBN: 978-1-5043-2931-6 (hc)
ISBN: 978-1-5043-2930-9 (e)

Library of Congress Control Number: 2015903681

Balboa Press rev. date: 5/22/2015

DEDICATION

With profound respect and gratitude I dedicate this
book to my friend, mentor, and soulmate, Mary Helen
Brownell. Through her gentle loving guidance, she literally
taught me how to open my heart and love again.

"If you want to awaken all of humanity, then awaken all of yourself. If you want to eliminate the suffering in the world, then eliminate all that is dark and negative in yourself. Truly, the greatest gift you have to give is that of your own self-transformation."
— Lao Tsu

CONTENTS

Preface xv
Acknowledgments xvii

Chapter 1:   Awakened Living 1

Enlightenment Is Our Natural State 1
Our True Nature 3
Disengaging the Mind 4
The Illusion of Separateness 6
The Truth about Karma 7
Shining Our Light 8
Un-Awakened Living 9
Clear Signs of Un-Awakened Living 10
Clear Signs of Awakened Living 10
Watch Your Language 11
Awakened Living Spiritual Community 12

Chapter 2:   Everyday Compassion 15

My First Teacher 15
An Act of Compassion 17

Mary Helen's Seven Spiritual Truths 19

   1) There's nothing "wrong" with you 19

   2) There's only one of us here 20

   3) The only prayer is thank you 21

   4) God is within you 22

   5) Nothing outside of you needs to change 23

   6) Everyone is perfect, just as they are 24

   7) We're not here to get good…only to become real 25

Living These Spiritual Truths 26

Chapter 3:   Remembering Our Wholeness 29

What Is Wholeness? 29

Unlearning 31

The Root of Addiction 32

The Shadow Self 33

Integrating the Shadow 34

Spiritual Bypass 36

Self-Forgiveness 36

Moving Beyond Limitation 37

Expanding Consciousness 38

Awakening Happens Now 39

The Value of Spiritual Community 40

Chapter 4:   Conscious Evolution 43

Levels of Consciousness 43

Level 1: Martyr State of Consciousness 44

  - Powerlessness and Addiction 45

  - The Causal Point of Change 46

Level 2: Magical Thinking Consciousness 47
Level 3: Metaphysical Consciousness 49
  - Self-Love 50
Level 4: Mystical Consciousness 51
  - Trusting the Process 52
The God Idea 53
Recognizing Your Level 55
Tools for Spiritual Unfolding 56
Sane or Insane? 57
A Call to Action 58

Chapter 5: Heaven on Earth 59

Collective Influence 59
Changing Paradigms 60
The Old Paradigm 61
Hell on Earth 64
Recognizing Illusion 65
Crumbling Structures 67
Disorientation 68
Heaven on Earth 69
Spiritual Teachers 70
Freedom from Addiction 71
Personal Accountability 72

Chapter 6: Awake Within the Dream 73

The Persistence of Illusion 73
Glimpses into Ultimate Reality 74
The Power of Perspective 76
Blessing or Curse? 77
Evidence or Conclusion? 78

Death and Rebirth 80
Leaning In 81
Fear of Dying 82
Serving Others 83

Chapter 7:   Living on Purpose 87

Doing and Being 87
Inner and Outer Purpose 88
Head and Heart..89
Knowing Our Outer Purpose..91
Nurturing Our Purpose 92
Purposeful Living 94
Right Brain Magnificence 95

Chapter 8:   Finding True Love 97

Love Is What We Are..97
The Search for Romantic Love 98
The Great Remembering 100
Support for Your Undoing 101
The Ultimate Observer 102
Living Beyond Our Stories..103
The Shortcut..105
A Deeper Look at Self-Love 106

Chapter 9:   True Abundance 109

Forgiveness 109
Getting It Right..111
Prosperity or Abundance?..113
The Seduction of the Ego..114

Look Back but Don't Stare 116
Security...116
Divine Integration 117

Chapter 10: Shift Happens 119

Reframing..119
Making U-turns...121
Trusting Our Inner Guide 122
A Shift from Ego to Spirit.. 123
Everything Is Love or a Request for Love 125
Time in the Wilderness 125
Acceptance and Denial 127
The Shift Is Internal 128

Chapter 11: An Ever-Changing World 131

Embracing Change 131
Pain and Suffering..133
Loving or Changing? 134
Paradigm of Oneness 137
Competition or Cooperation? 138
Our Unique Journeys 139

Chapter 12: Now What? 141

Courage to Change 141
Living in the Question 142
Concepts and Ideologies 143
Spiritual Inquiry 143
What Is The Valuable Question?................................144
The Opinion Trap 145

Not Knowing 146
The Hundredth Monkey..147
One Life 148
The New Meditation 148
A Greater Reality 149

Index...151

PREFACE

It is with immeasurable respect and gratitude that I present this book. It has been 10 years in the making. Not that I have been writing this book for all those years, but because my own journey over the past decade has prepared me for sharing this message with you. In 2005, I had the calling to move into what I now know is my life's work. I listened to my inner-knowing and set out on a course of spiritual exploration beyond what I could have ever imagined.

During those years, my spiritual path took me to the highest highs, and the lowest lows. I have been propelled from darkness to light; from shame to acceptance; separation to oneness; and ultimately to an indescribable sense of personal freedom. After many years of clinging and aversion, I find myself today resting in a greater reality; a deeper experience of joy than I ever knew possible. It has delivered me to this moment and a profound understanding of my true purpose.

I have awakened to my true nature.

It is my sincere honor to share what I have discovered.

Life is a great experiment, and my role is not to provide anybody with definitive answers, but rather to open up questions and engage humanity in a conversation about awakening to our highest potential. My invitation is that you explore the mystical concepts put forward in this book, try them on, and see what happens. After all, my words are meaningless unless they point you to a way of being that brings you increased joy, love, and peace.

It has been said, the only way to speak authentically about spirituality is to speak in paradox. So, you may well read ideas that appear to be contradictory in the pages of this book. In order to include the whole of your experience, you ought to realize that there is a wide spectrum of perspectives that exist at any given moment, in any given situation—from human reality to spiritual truth.

All My Love, TJ

ACKNOWLEDGMENTS

A special thanks to the spiritual teachers, and all who have—directly or indirectly—been instrumental in the process of writing this book.

I offer deep appreciation for the dynamic teachings of Rev. Maureene Bass and the grounded, mystical presence of Rev. Dr. Joan Steadman.

Additionally, I want to honor the spiritual teachers and authors who have been influential to my work, especially: Eckhart Tolle, Pema Chodron, and Byron Katie.

And, of course, I extend deep gratitude to the amazing inspiration of Oprah.

Also, a sincere thank you for the support of the Awakened Living folks, Alison, Brian, Carsten, Jess, Kristin, Sahina, and Summer.

Finally, a special thanks to my family and friends who have supported me, especially Gregory, Susan, Gwen, Kealoha, Chet, John and Joel. And heartfelt gratitude to my loving partner, Will Griffin, for his unyielding love and support, and for helping me to open my heart to a deeper level of love and intimacy than I have ever known.

Editorial Assistance
Developmental Editor: Sahina Grinczer
Editor: Jim Gebbie

Chapter One

AWAKENED LIVING

"Knowing yourself goes far deeper than the adoption of a set of ideas or beliefs. Spiritual ideas and beliefs may at best be helpful pointers. But in themselves, they rarely have the power to dislodge the more firmly established core concepts of who you think you are, which are part of the conditioning of the human mind. Knowing yourself deeply has nothing to do with whatever ideas are floating around in your mind. Knowing yourself is to be rooted in Being, instead of lost in your mind."
— *Excerpt from* A New Earth, *by Eckhart Tolle*

Enlightenment Is Our Natural State

It is the birthright of each and every one of us to live an awakened life. Most religions and spiritual traditions teach us that we need to adopt a certain belief system or follow some prescribed steps in order to attain a state of enlightenment. A long-held belief about awakening is that only a small number of people, destined to become gurus or spiritual teachers, can attain it. It is certainly true that until recent times only a small minority of people on the planet had attained this state of full self-realization. These saints, mystics, and spiritual masters were seen as "special." And they certainly were, at the time. However, times are changing.

We are now living in an era of rapid acceleration of the phenomenon of spiritual awakening. The truth is that awakening is absolutely available to every single human being on the planet right here, right now. Enlightenment is our most natural state. When we strip away all the concepts and ideas we have learned over our lifetime—about ourselves and how we view the world—we uncover the simple truth. We discover who we have always been—pure consciousness. Before the accumulation of ideas, we were pure awareness. We are still pure awareness. This awareness simply witnesses life, as it unfolds, through and around us. There is nothing we need to do, or believe, to become enlightened. We simply remember who we essentially are. We already are that which we seek.

I recently heard a beautiful story that illustrates this. The story was related to me by a friend who knew a young couple who had just birthed their second baby. They noticed that their older child, then four years of age, was sneaking into the newborn's room at night. Curious what the four-year-old was up to, they decided to install a video camera in the baby's room so they could observe what was happening. To their surprise, they discovered the older child was visiting the baby and asking it: "Please tell me about God...I'm beginning to forget." This child had the awareness that his innate sense of wholeness was already slipping away. And he realized that the baby was capable of reminding him of what he was forgetting.

Enlightenment is actually a very ordinary state. It is also an extra-ordinary state. It feels elevated because it is not burdened by all the weighty ideas and beliefs we had previously amassed. When we come to realize the truth of who and what we are, we are no longer limited by the false sense of identity we had previously been confined within. Our natural state of freedom is restored. There is no longer anything to fear. The deep peace of our true nature is revealed to us. We are no longer run by the programs in our mind—that is, our learned ideas about who we are and how we "should" live, including our concepts of "right and wrong," and "good and bad." We have remembered that we are pure consciousness. Consciousness inherently knows itself. It knows that everything exists *within it*. Knowing itself, it is naturally benevolent. It is not against anything. It knows itself *as* everything. When we are fully self-realized, we naturally speak and act *as* love. We could not possibly do anything else.

Our True Nature

Experiencing ourselves as love is the most natural thing in the world. The path to remembering ourselves as love is one of dismantling or unlearning everything we have been taught that contradicts this truth. Self-realization is nothing more than coming into alignment with what we already inherently are. Throughout our lives, we have received messages that taught us otherwise. Often at a young age, we come to the conclusion that we are less than whole and perfect, that we are less than love. For the most part, children believe the messages they hear. That is because their minds have not yet developed the analytical ability to question them. Even though some messages don't feel right intuitively, a young, undeveloped mind cannot help but believe what it is told, especially when it is a repeated message. This creates a distorted or false self-image. It's like looking into one of those funhouse mirrors that pulls one's image way out of shape. When, as children, we received feedback that we were bad, that there was something wrong with us, that we were lacking in some way, it's as though we were looking at a distorted reflection and believing it to be true.

The messages that created a false self-image might have come from family members, friends, school teachers, or other authority figures that we assumed were wiser than us. These messages continue as we grow into adulthood, getting layered upon and often reinforcing those messages we received as children. However, when we wake up to the reality of who we are, we see that we were given those messages by people who were themselves living in a state of forgetfulness about their true identity. They were not capable of always mirroring an accurate reflection to us.

As we remember our true identity, we realize that all of our experiences have been part of our journey from unconsciousness to consciousness. There is nobody to blame. Everything happened exactly as it did. We have been part of the evolution of consciousness, waking up to itself. We have experienced darkness in order that we can experience light. Without darkness, we cannot appreciate light. Darkness has no power. It is merely absence of light.

Disengaging the Mind

The realization of our true nature can happen in an instant. It can happen at any moment. However, often when we catch a glimpse of it, our mind quickly reasserts itself. Sometimes we experience a prolonged state of wakefulness before our mind takes back its control. These glimpses of our natural state arise in the space between our thoughts. They happen the moment we stop identifying with our thoughts. The shift of focus, from the content of our mind to the space in which our thoughts arise, is the shift from separation to oneness. No matter what we are thinking, thought is thought. Awareness is not affected by thought. It is the screen on which thought appears. As long as we identify with our thoughts, we are identified with what is changing and temporary. With a shift of focus, we can shift our identity to what is changeless and permanent.

It is often said that the only thing we can rely on is change. This is certainly true if our focus is solely on the physical dimension of life, which includes our mental and emotional states. Everything physical is subject to change. And our thoughts and emotions are subject to change. We are currently experiencing more rapid change in our lives than ever before. Our jobs, relationships, finances, and living situations are all less stable than they once were. It is evident that security cannot be found in external circumstances. But when we shift our focus to what is changeless—awareness itself—we can experience the only true security there is. When we cultivate an awareness of witness consciousness, we are in touch with what is eternal.

When I was in my late 30s, I lost everything I had worked so hard to achieve. Without much warning, everything I had strived for and accumulated was gone. Despite feeling devastated, one of the gifts of this experience was that I no longer had anything left to lose. Therefore I had no reason to fear loss of anything. From this experience, I was able to separate out my true self from my material possessions and from the circumstances of my life. I was aware of the "I" that did not change when everything around me completely changed. I decided that if I were going to rebuild my life, I was going to do it from the inside out, not the outside in. I knew that everything outside of me could be taken away in an instant. I had to find a way of recognizing my true foundation. In his book, *The Second Book of the Tao*, Stephen Mitchell states, "*The master knows that in looking forward there are endless possibilities, but looking backwards, there's only one.*" The truth of this statement became vividly clear to me when I was no longer identified with the things that change in my life.

The Illusion of Separateness

We have all been conditioned to divide our experiences into "good and bad," or "right and wrong," as illustrated in the following analogy. Say I am rowing a boat down a river and another boat hits mine. If I look over and see that nobody is in the other boat, nobody is to blame for what happened. But if my boat is hit by another boat and I look over and see someone in that boat, my conditioned mind immediately blames that person for my experience. My ego wants to make the other person responsible for "what they did to me." However, from a different perspective—a perspective of oneness— that other person is part of the natural world, part of the oneness of life. He is no guiltier than nature itself. When we stop dividing the world into "us and them," there is no longer anyone to blame for our uncomfortable experiences. We take full responsibility for how we respond to life.

If we take an honest look at our lives, right now, we can allow ourselves to see where we divide our world into "us and them" or "right and wrong." In other words we can see where we hold prejudice or judgment about others. It then becomes clear how we create every single division or separation in the world we inhabit. We create it with the power of our thinking. When we believe these thoughts, the division feels real. When we believe it's real, our system generates emotions to match the beliefs. We assume our emotion is confirmation of the truth of our belief. But our belief creates the emotion. This is how we create our individualized reality. It's how we create feelings of superiority and inferiority, the desire to blame or harm another, feelings of hatred or fear of a perceived other.

Attaining enlightenment requires that we be willing to examine and make an honest appraisal of our thinking. It's possible to discover the lens through which we are seeing life. It entails accepting what we find and working with it. There is a certain familiarity and comfort about continuing to perceive the world the way we have always perceived it. It can be difficult, and sometimes painful to confront the darker aspects of ourselves. But, we can claim more of our light only by being willing to walk through the dark and uncomfortable places we encounter within—not by avoiding them or trying to maneuver around them. The only way out is through.

The Truth about Karma

Karma is not an outside force. It is repetitively thinking the same idea about ourselves and about the world and getting the same results. It feels like it's coming from outside us. In actuality, we are imprinting our thoughts, attitudes, intentions, and beliefs—whether they are conscious or unconscious—upon the world, and receiving them back in return. If we believe that we are fundamentally flawed or inferior, then life will seem to reflect that reality back to us. We will see it in our circumstances, and in the people we encounter and what they choose to say to us. If we are convinced that we don't deserve, or are not capable, life will seem to confirm that to be true. That will happen again and again until we change the program or the lens through which we are looking. If we feel confident and know that we can achieve our highest goals, our belief and corresponding actions will allow that to be reflected back to us in our lives.

I sometimes see people coming into the New Thought or New Age movement and simply "redressing" old concepts and calling them new. The idea of a "cosmic 2x4" is a perfect example of this. A cosmic 2x4 is seen as the universe sending us a message or teaching us a lesson when we do not properly surrender. People simply change the name of a punishing God to something that sounds different. I am not saying that life does not present us with growth opportunities in the form of difficulty. I am just offering the possibility that it is not an outside force "doing this" to us. It is more about a way of coming into alignment with our true nature.

Each of us is accountable for how we view our world. Nobody else has the power to change the internal workings of our minds and hearts. However, surrounding ourselves with people who support and encourage our evolving perspective can be enormously powerful. It is comparable to planting ourselves in fertile soil that nurtures our growth. The world in which we live is a world of our own making. The world does not actually exist "out there." The relationship we have with our world is the relationship we have created in our minds. No other world exists. The world we perpetuate is the world we perpetuate in our minds. It is also the world we model for others who live within our field of influence. When we choose to step into the reality of oneness, we immediately inhabit that world of connectedness with all things, based on love. That world already exists, within us, and it is available to us at any given moment. We choose it—or not—moment to moment. We show love by being conscious of the words and actions we use to respond to life, in the present moment. If we are not awake enough to consciously choose our response, an unconscious or automatic response, based on our past conditioning, will emerge and dictate the conditions of our lives.

Shining Our Light

To enlighten means to "shine light upon." When we are living an awakened life, rather than looking for love outside ourselves, we live *as* light, *as* love. Each of us has this innate ability to shine light and love upon any situation we encounter that lacks it, that is in need of it. In the awakened state, we are no longer waiting for someone or something outside us to provide the light or love we have been seeking. No matter what situation we find ourselves in, when we have remembered who we truly are—consciousness itself—we naturally shine our light upon that which we witness. From this place, we no longer play a victim role. We know ourselves to be inviolable.

As witness consciousness, we understand that not everyone has yet awakened to the reality of who they are. We may be around others who have not yet realized their freedom to choose the kind of world in which they live. We know that we always maintain our freedom to choose—and that it is not for us to impose our choice on others. Each of us arrives at self-realization in our own time. Once we have fully arrived there ourselves, we have a natural, compassionate understanding for those who have not. By radiating our light, we serve as a reminder and an inspiration to others who have not yet remembered their true essence.

Un-Awakened Living

When we have forgotten the truth of who and what we are, we are living unconsciously. Our thoughts and behaviors are taken over by the old habits, patterns, and conditioning of our past. We lose our freedom of choice in how to respond to life. When we are not awake to our true nature, we can be easily triggered by the behavior and words of others and by our circumstances. These moments of discomfort and reactivity can be seen as alarm bells. They remind us to "wake up to who and what we are." When we allow our upset feelings and emotional hurts to become our "allies," we stay on track. It helps remind us that we can shift into the witness position, rather than identifying with any drama that is happening. Instead of getting pulled in by the details of our "human story," we can choose to be the one shining light on any given circumstance.

Clear Signs of Un-Awakened Living

- blaming others for our unwanted experiences
- judging people or situations as "right/wrong," or "good/bad"
- wanting to control others
- feeling superior or inferior
- experiencing resistance to what is
- getting emotionally triggered by what others are saying or doing
- needing to express opinions

Clear Signs of Awakened Living

- experiencing oneness and connection
- choosing acceptance and understanding
- feeling comfortable in our "skin"
- understanding a deep sense of belonging
- expressing authenticity and vulnerability
- being unattached to outcomes
- knowing a deep sense of purpose

Living an awakened life is a moment-to-moment experience, which becomes more stabilized over time. There are times when we know ourselves to be pure love, light, and peace, beyond all shadow of a doubt. And there are other moments when we get emotionally triggered and old habits kick in. In that moment, we have forgotten who and what we are. These moments of forgetting are like dark clouds passing over the sun. They are temporary. The sun is still shining behind the clouds; it is just obscured. We can trust that our clarity will return. Behind the clouds of unconscious thought, our clear perception always remains. Our essential self will always be there when the passing clouds have dispersed. As witness consciousness, we have compassion for ourselves even when the clouds appear.

In Jiddu Krishnamurti's words: "The highest form of human intelligence is to observe yourself without judgment." When we can do this, we are truly free.

Watch Your Language

There are some words in the English language that, when used, immediately take us out of an awakened state, or prevent us from finding it in the first place. I have found the following practice to be helpful:

Make a list of 5-10 words that do not support your awakened state or that seem to separate you from your consciousness. Make a commitment to become aware of using these words and eliminate them from your vocabulary. The intention of the practice is to stop using them altogether. I have attended workshops where it is suggested you wear a rubber band on your wrist and "flick" it when you hear yourself saying the words. Personally, I suggest a softer, gentler approach. Use a heightened level of awareness to recognize these words, and their effect on you and your world. My current chosen words are: *should, must, good, bad, right,* and *wrong.* When you use words like these, believing them to be true, the result is black-and-white thinking. We create a world divided into rigid compartments, excluding parts of the whole. And, it is always possible to find replacement words that support your spiritual awakening and support a more loving way of being in the world. Those words can help you live the life you want.

Bringing awareness to how we create our reality with our thoughts and words is a vital step in transforming our perspective of the world. When I hear myself using the words listed above, I think to myself, "Oh, there I go again." And I remember that I don't have to believe what I'm thinking. When I observe myself having thoughts like: "What's wrong with me?" or "He should..." or "She must..." I experience how those words immediately separate me. Those thoughts take me from that place of awareness, where I have a choice. We are always choosing, whether we realize it or not. As we continue to practice this, it becomes a natural way of being. Repetition strengthens and confirms this truth.

It has been said that you cannot un-raise consciousness. Once we have awakened to the fact that we create the world we live in, moment to moment, we can take responsibility for our thoughts and words. I am reminded that we are not responsible for our first thought, but we are responsible for what we do with it. Years of conditioning can be difficult to change. However, by bringing our awareness to what we are currently creating, we can begin to change our experience—if that is what we want. Changing our habits of thinking and speaking opens the door for a new world to be born, a world born within our consciousness.

Awakened Living Spiritual Community

Awakened Living is a 21st century movement in San Francisco for people who consider themselves spiritual, but not religious, and have a deep hunger for personal and global transformation. We meet for workshops, spiritual gatherings, and interactive groups with the deliberate intention of making our lives deeply fulfilling while creating a more peaceful and loving world. Our mission is to encourage and inspire the awakening of human consciousness.

People often ask me, "What is the basic teaching of Awakened Living?" My first response is that there isn't necessarily a basic teaching. However, at its core Awakened Living recognizes we are one with source, one with God, one with light, and one with love. That fundamental understanding revolutionarily changes our lives, in dramatic ways. Many of us grew up in religions that taught us there was a source outside ourselves. We needed to surrender to it, or we needed to learn how to understand a particular teaching in order to *be* OK. At Awakened Living, our fundamental knowing is that we are one with this power. That understanding changes our lives in significant ways.

It seems that in many traditional religions there is an idea, somehow, that we are inherently broken. We feel there's something wrong with us, and we are looking for salvation. What is different at Awakened Living is that we firmly believe we are whole, perfect and divine. And that it is not about us finding a way to attain anything. It is, however, discovering a way to "loosen" the grip of those things that oppose this truth.

Please visit us online at **www.awakenedlivingsf.org** for more information and to join our movement.

Chapter Two

EVERYDAY COMPASSION

"Compassion is not a relationship between the healer and the wounded. It's a relationship between equals. Only when we know our own darkness well can we be present with the darkness of others. Compassion becomes real when we recognize our shared humanity."
— *Excerpt from* When Thing Fall Apart, *by Pema Chodron*

My First Teacher

When I was 20 years old, I met a remarkable woman, named Mary Helen Brownell. Meeting her completely changed the course of my life. Mary Helen was the most compassionate human being I had ever encountered and she became my first spiritual teacher. By the time I met her, I had already built many layers of armor around my heart in order to feel safe in this world. Some difficult childhood and adolescent experiences had made me believe that I needed to carefully protect myself against further hurt. Mary Helen was able to see right through my emotional defenses, to the core of who I really was, beneath my protective facade. Because of her, and the trust I felt in her, I was able to open my heart and love again. My heartbreaking stories became a catalyst for *breaking my heart open* to a new way of being.

Mary Helen was born in Dallas, in 1923, into a wealthy family. She had a sheltered upbringing, living with her family in an affluent part of town. She told me that she did not realize that black people existed, apart from the family driver, until she went to college. She married and had children at a young age, doing her best to conform to the traditional lifestyle that was expected of her. For Mary Helen, however, there was a deep yearning to follow her inner knowing and forge her own path. As with many enlightened beings, her early life was spent struggling with her "demons" and her ego. After many years of trying to conform to an inauthentic expression of her life, she sank into a period of deep unhappiness and turned to drugs and alcohol and lived the life of an alcoholic and addict until 1957, when she became involved in the recovery movement. After several more years of struggling with her addictions, and spending time in and out of mental institutions, she was finally able to get and stay sober from 1967 until her passing in July of 1998.

In the 1970s Mary Helen became a counselor at a treatment program that served soldiers who were coming home from the Vietnam War. She spent hundreds, if not thousands, of hours sitting with men who had returned home suffering from severe war trauma. Her own personal struggle with addictions had prepared her well for this work. She was able to understand that the difficulties these traumatized men were experiencing were a direct result of them losing the ability to connect with the essential truth of who they really were, at the level of spirit. A large part of her work entailed addressing what stood in the way of her clients realizing the truth of their being. Mary Helen devoted the rest of her life to helping people recover from addictions. It was through her counseling work that I met her, at the time in my life when I was struggling with my own addictions. She helped me get sober, and literally saved my life. And for that, I am eternally grateful. She also taught me how to access my inner-wisdom and love again.

An Act of Compassion

In her later life, Mary Helen was a student of Eastern philosophy, studying the writings of Paramahansa Yogananda, Swami Sivananda, and other Indian spiritual masters. She became a devotee of Sathya Sai Baba and took many trips to India, making pilgrimages there for many years. One of my most memorable moments with Mary Helen occurred when I accompanied her on one of these trips, back in 1992. On that trip, I saw a deeply touching example of her everyday compassion. We were at the Los Angeles airport, at the beginning of our journey. Due to one of Mary Helen's health issues, we needed to wait for medical clearance, which meant a 24-hour delay. The rest of our group had taken an earlier flight, and we decided to make the most of our delay-time at the airport, finding ways to entertain ourselves. Suddenly, a young mother and her baby became the focus of our attention. The baby was crying at full volume, while its mother, unable to control the screaming, became increasingly frustrated and agitated. Her unsuccessful attempts to console the baby led to her yelling and verbally abusing the child. Everybody within an earshot now had their attention focused on the unfolding scene. People were visibly horrified at what they were witnessing.

I watched Mary Helen as she stood up, walked over to the young mother, and said, "Hi, it seems like you need some help. I was a young mother myself once, and I know how difficult it can be. Let me help you." Mary Helen took the baby out of the woman's arms and sat down next to her. While Mary Helen soothed the baby, the mother became tearful, obviously relieved to have help in her moment of need. I was aware of how everything shifted the moment Mary Helen had chosen to meet the situation with love, rather than resistance. The tension that had built up was immediately dissolved by her act of compassion. I do not know for sure whether that was the first response Mary Helen had to the alarming situation, but it was what she chose to express, from her place of loving openheartedness. After half an hour or so, Mary Helen stood up and walked back to me. No words were exchanged about what had happened. No words were necessary. But I knew that what I had just witnessed was a beautiful example of what is means to live an awakened life.

The above story is in sharp contrast to another mother-and-baby incident I recently witnessed as I was walking down Market Street in San Francisco. I saw a woman with her child, in a stroller, hurriedly pushing it down a flight of stairs, to a public transport station. She seemed to be putting the child's safety at risk. A passerby started shouting at her, "What kind of a mother are you? Are you crazy? You're endangering your child!" As I watched this scene, my mind flashed back to the incident at the Los Angeles airport with Mary Helen, and her very different response to a similar situation. Mary Helen had chosen "How may I help you?" rather than "How can I judge you?"

The moment-to-moment choices we make in our daily interactions with each other are what create the kind of world in which we live. By choosing to express compassion and understanding in the face of another's pain or struggle, rather than judgment or impatience, we change the emotional climate of the world. Every situation is an opportunity to open up or to close off. One of my favorite definitions of a spiritual experience is "a profound alteration in our reaction to life." Actually I would change that to "a profound alteration in our *response* to life."

Mary Helen's Seven Spiritual Truths

What I learned from being in the presence of Mary Helen formed the foundation of my spiritual understanding. I have summarized what she taught me in the following seven principles. These spiritual truths are the basis of what I consider to be essential guidance for awakened living.

1) *There's nothing "wrong" with you*

Mary Helen used to say to me, in her beautiful southern accent, "Darlin', you're so precious." She said it to me so many times that one day I started to actually believe it. She literally loved me into a new way of seeing myself and a new way of being. Until we can look at someone and see the perfection that is at their core, we are not seeing them clearly. As humans, we all carry some unhealed emotional wounds within us. We all have some weaknesses of personality along with our strengths and gifts. However, if we identify ourselves or others with limitations or unresolved issues—rather than with the essential goodness and wholeness that is within each of us—then we are only seeing at a superficial level.

In traditional addiction recovery programs, people are asked to repeatedly affirm their identity as *being* their addiction. I would like to suggest that it might be more beneficial and healing for addicts to repeatedly affirm their inherent perfection. I am not suggesting that anyone be in denial about their addictive behavior. It is a vital step to acknowledge and name that which we wish to change about ourselves. But I do want to point to the higher truth of our essential identity, which is our inherent wholeness. Another common practice is to focus on "defects of character" which need to be removed. I would like to offer a different perspective. It has been said that defects are simply assets with the volume turned up too high. In those terms, the conversation shifts to balancing traits rather than removing "defects." In my experience, this is not only a gentler relationship to self, but a far more effective one. Repeating a negative affirmation, sometimes for years on end and continually referring to oneself as a disease or seeing oneself as defective, has the potential for producing a negative impact on one's self-image and life. I am grateful to be part of the creation of a new paradigm in treatment where this positive focus is becoming more accepted and celebrated.

The gift of any spiritual teacher is that he or she knows, beyond any shadow of a doubt, that perfection is at the core of each and every person. A spiritual teacher is anyone who has absolutely come to know their own true identity as pure love, light, and wholeness. Living an awakened life means knowing that our essential wholeness can never be lost, even though it might be covered over or seemingly forgotten. Our wholeness, the source of unconditional love within, is always available to be revealed to us, as the ultimate truth of who we are.

2) *There's only one of us here*

There is a lot of talk these days about oneness. Many people have caught on to the idea that everything is interconnected; that at some level, humanity is all one. All that exists is one. But how many of us really *know* that—and *live* it? And *how* do we live from oneness? I have a practice I find useful when I am feeling triggered, shut down, or resistant. Rather than seeing *the other* as doing the thing that triggers or irritates me, I say to myself, "Isn't it interesting that *I'm* doing that?" I recognize that if we are one, then *I'm doing the thing that irritates me*. I invite you to try this yourself for the next 24 hours. See every single person you encounter as yourself. Think of yourself and the other as "us" or "we" rather than seeing a separate "you" or "they." Notice what happens, and how it changes your response to both seemingly negative *and* positive behaviors in others. What happens to your emotional and physical state? What happens to your world view? What happens to how you experience life?

3) *The only prayer is thank you*

Prayer is often seen as asking for something or asking for something to be removed. But, in many ways, asking is affirming lack consciousness. If we ask for something, we affirm that we are not already whole and complete and that getting something is needed. Asking for something to be removed is affirming that there is something wrong with *what is*. It may seem insignificant, but when we simply shift from "please" to "thank you," everything changes. When we shift our perspective to gratitude, infinite possibilities open up in our lives.

When we are in touch with the wholeness and fullness of who we truly are—when we see things from the mystical level described in more detail in a following chapter, there is nothing left to seek, externally or internally. We are already all that we need to be. This moment, right now, contains everything we need. The intention is to stop seeking happiness. Seeking is the antithesis of happiness, because we already *have* and we already *are* everything we believe we need.

The more we tap into our natural gratitude, the more life seems to give us to be grateful for. As a practice, I invite you to infuse your day with gratitude—for both the "good" *and* the so-called "bad." It is easy enough to be grateful for seeing the beautiful smile of a child, or for receiving a gift, but what about feeling gratitude for being stuck in traffic? Or losing something you valued? What happens when you start saying yes to *all* of your experiences, trusting that all of it is as it "should" be? Say thank you in order to come into alignment with *what is*, and live in gratitude. My current practice of this principle often involves repeating, "Thank you, God," or "Thank you, Universe," out loud throughout the day regarding *every* situation in my life.

4) *God is within you*

Mary Helen often said to me: "You know, God is within you, and when you listen carefully, that inner voice will guide you. There's no power outside you that you need to surrender to." Now, given that the context was said in Dallas, back in the 1980s, this was a revolutionary idea at the time. The general consensus in that particular culture was that God was a man who lived in the sky. For Mary Helen to declare that this all-powerful force, the source of all creation, was inside us was groundbreaking. It took me a while to get comfortable saying this one. People usually misunderstand the notion in saying, "I am God." They interpreted it through the ego. She was not saying, "I'm God, and you are not." Rather, she was acknowledging that everyone on the planet is an expression of the source energy from which all of life emanates. And because of that, we all have direct access to the love, intelligence, and guidance of that source, from within.

In my current state of consciousness, I would modify this, by saying that we *are* this power, rather than saying God is within us.

We are each perfect expressions of the one power and one presence. This may seem like semantics, but saying God is within us, implies that there is a separate God that is within you like a "wiener in a bun," as my friend and teacher Rev. Dr. Paul Hasselbeck so brilliantly states.

The Rumi quote—"*You are not a drop in the ocean. You are the entire ocean in a drop*" illustrates this beautifully.

5) *Nothing outside of you needs to change*

From the perspective of the metaphysical and mystical Levels, (described in more detail in Chapter Four) nothing outside of us needs to change in order for us to be happy. The world is unfolding perfectly, moment to moment. If we feel resistance or unhappiness about anything, all we need to change is our view or our relationship to it in order to be at peace. I am not suggesting that anyone be in denial about what they feel or need to say, or that they should not take action they feel called to take. What I *am* pointing to is the higher truth that our happiness is not dependent on anything outside ourselves needing to change. Happiness is always available to us *right now*. We all know how futile it is to attempt to change others. But, we are also *always* choosing how we see others, and how we view the world in general. Interestingly, when we change our perspective about the person who irritates us, or a challenging circumstance, then that person or circumstance seems to change before our very eyes. A Course in Miracles states: "*The greatest capacity we have for changing the world is to change our mind about the world.*"

What we are really talking about here is making friends with impermanence. Building sandcastles is a good metaphor here. Anyone who has ever built a sandcastle knows that the tide eventually comes in and washes it away. But that does not take away our desire to build it, or our enjoyment in doing so. In the same way, we honor our desire and need to live our lives—to build a career, have relationships, and plan for our future—while also realizing that none of these things ultimately bring us lasting happiness. In the end, it all gets washed away by the tides of life. The only thing that does not get erased is our oneness with source, our identity *as* source.

6) *Everyone is perfect, just as they are*

When I first met Mary Helen, I would often go to her feeling frustrated about the way people around me were behaving. In my 20-year-old perspective, I believed the person I was having a problem with "should" be acting differently. Mary Helen would respond with "Well, if you had their life experience, you would be exactly as they are. They're being the perfect _____ " (filling in the blank with the name of the person with whom I was upset). Seeing things through her eyes taught me how to adjust the lens through which I was looking. Once I cleared my own vision, I too could see that they were being the perfect version of themselves. My judgment gradually gave way to more compassion and understanding, for myself and for others. Another simple, yet powerful tool she offered was to imagine a cord connecting me to everyone I knew. Then, I was to imagine a large pair of scissors gently cutting the cord that connected us. I did this every night before I want to sleep for many months. This allowed me to disengage from my thoughts about and seeming entanglements with others. It allowed me to gently shift the focus of attention to myself and my own spiritual journey.

7) *We're not here to get good…only to become real*

One of Mary Helen's favorite readings was the following excerpt from *The Velveteen Rabbit*, by Margery Williams:

> *"What is REAL?" asked the Velveteen Rabbit, one day. "Does it mean having things that buzz inside you and a stick-out handle?"*
>
> *"Real isn't how you are made," said the Skin Horse. "It's a thing that happens to you. When a child loves you for a long, long time, not just to play with, but REALLY loves you, then you become real."*
>
> *"Does it hurt?" asked the Rabbit.*
>
> *"Sometimes," said the Skin Horse, for he was always truthful. "But, when you are Real, you don't mind being hurt."*
>
> *"Does it happen all at once, like being wound up," asked the Rabbit, "or bit by bit?"*
>
> *"It doesn't happen all at once," said the Skin Horse. "You become. It takes a long time. That's why it doesn't often happen to people who break easily or have sharp edges, or who have been carefully kept. Generally, by the time you are Real, most of your hair has been loved off, your eyes drop out, and you get loose in your joints, and very shabby. But these things don't matter at all because once you are Real, you can't be ugly—except to people who don't understand."*

> *"I suppose you are real?" asked the Rabbit. And then he wished he hadn't said that for he thought the Skin Horse might be sensitive. But the Skin Horse only smiled.*
>
> *"The boy's uncle made me real," he said. "That was many years ago. But once you are real, you cannot become unreal again. It lasts for always."*

Many people in the world believe they have the "right" way to do things. Many religions teach that their way is *the* way. And, if we can just follow these rules and be "good," we will find happiness (or at least get into heaven). Mary Helen so beautifully taught me, mostly by example, that becoming real is far more important than being "good." She was a perfect example of the principles of authenticity and vulnerability which have become the foundation of my life's work.

Living These Spiritual Truths

It has been said, "*The spiritual life is not a theory; we have to live it.*" The above seven spiritual concepts may sound simple—and they are. However, it is only when we *live* them in our everyday lives that they make any lasting difference. In those moments when we are in reaction to something that someone just said or did… can we remember that "there's only one of us here," or that "she's being the perfect Susan," or that "nothing outside of me needs to change"? When we are feeling lost or confused…can we trust that if we sit quietly and go within, we might just find the answer we are looking for? When we are suffering from the effects of our own self-judgment and criticisms, what might happen if we remember that "there's nothing *wrong* with me"?

My invitation for you as you move throughout your day is to shine as much light of your awareness as you can onto the moment-to-moment choices you are making. It has been said that heaven and hell are states that exist within you. They are both available to everybody, at any given moment. The state you find yourself in is dependent on the myriad daily choices you make. You have the power to change the lens through which you view the world—and therefore to change your experience *of* the world, which always exists within your consciousness.

I believe this is what Jesus was referring to when he said: *"Be in this world, but not of it."*

Chapter Three

REMEMBERING OUR WHOLENESS

"What all of us most want is the experience of our own essential nature. This yearning is behind every worldly desire. When we are out of contact with our own essence, we look for fulfillment from the world. To fulfill our desires, we develop a strategy that requires repressing some aspect of ourselves because that quality appears to be the threat to the fulfillment of our desires."

— *Excerpt from* Birthing a Greater Reality, *by Robert Brumet*

What Is Wholeness?

Our wholeness, our essential nature, is who we are without all the false identities we have accumulated throughout or lives. Finding our wholeness is a matter of letting go of all the illusory ideas we have accumulated about ourselves. These ideas have created a false, limited sense of self, known as our ego. Recovering our wholeness, therefore, involves allowing these illusory notions to dissolve so that our inherent, pristine self can be revealed. There is nothing we need to add. Nothing we need to acquire. Nothing we need to learn. Nothing we need to do. We are *already* whole and perfect. Life is not about learning, it is about unlearning all the stories we have believed about ourselves and the world. Asking ourselves the question "What do I need to let go of?" will take us in the right direction. As the saying goes, "When life isn't adding up—start subtracting."

There is a Hindu story that I heard while I was staying in an ashram in India. The story portrays God as talking to his students. They are asking Him, "Where shall we hide you? Shall we hide you in the depths of the ocean? Or perhaps we could hide you in the highest star!" The students come up with many different ideas about where to hide God, so that he won't be easily discovered by human beings. And God says, "No, no…I know where to hide myself! I'll hide myself deep within the heart of every human being. That's the last place they will think to look!"

Forgetting our wholeness is at the root of all our problems, struggles, conflicts, and crises. It is inevitable that we grow up learning to see the world—and ourselves—through the eyes of our primary caretakers and the influential adults in our lives. Along with all the necessary information about life, a lot of false information is also downloaded into our young minds. This happened long before we developed the ability to analyze the incoming data and decide what we want to take in and what we do not. Our subconscious mind is therefore programmed, from the very beginning, by the environment we are born into. Whether we want it or not, as children, we inherit the belief systems, perspectives, stories, and traditions of our family and of the culture in which we were raised. This downloaded information forms a kind of cultural operating system in our minds.

In the process of growing up and individuating, we differentiate ourselves from our family members, to a certain degree. Much of our unconscious programming remains intact for the rest of our lives. However, we can begin to question it and do the important inner work of releasing those aspects of our conditioning that no longer serve our highest good. This involves becoming conscious of the lens through which we are viewing the world. We might ask ourselves whether we are in agreement with that view. First we need to become conscious of the ingrained habits of mind that cause us to judge, to have prejudice, to be fearful when there is no reason to be, to think in limited ways—about ourselves, others, and the world in general. Once identified, we can evaluate these inherited habits of thinking. Are they true or useful for us? Do they come from a loving, openhearted place or a closed-hearted, fearful one? If we have outgrown those patterns, attitudes, and actions, we can let them go, trusting in this natural process of updating our beliefs and perspectives.

Unlearning

An important part of my work with individuals, as a spiritual coach, addiction counselor and minister, involves helping them uncover unconscious beliefs they have adopted. It also involves discovering decisions they made about themselves, usually as young children, which are creating the issues they are currently experiencing. Even though they have reached adulthood, they retain the belief systems and decisions they made as children. Those early learnings still shape their inner experience, as well as the outer events in their lives.

I remember coming to the conclusion, when I was a child, that I was not "good enough." As a young adult going out into the world, this story about myself was repeatedly mirrored back to me in different situations. Each time it seemed to confirm my belief that it was true. I learned, however, that our outer lives are a projection of our inner reality, our beliefs and attitudes. These get played out in our daily experiences. As long as we continue to believe in the concepts of separation, lack, and fear, they will indeed appear to be "real." Our lives will validate what we hold to be true. Conversely, if we begin to see life as abundant, rewarding, and delightful, they will also appear to be real. And our lives will take shape to validate those experiences. Until I recognized my life was being created 100 percent by what I was projecting, I could not experience true freedom. Releasing our false notions about ourselves and about life in general is how we uncover the deeper, essential truth that will set us free.

Spiritual psychology recognizes the existence of the transcendent aspect of human beings, as well as the separate, physical self. It encompasses the full range of our existence, rather than merely the visible, human aspect. This enables us to integrate the different aspects of ourselves into a whole. Just like two sides of the same coin, our transcendent or spiritual self and our earthly, human self—although apparently diametrically opposed to each other—are intrinsically one and the same. They are the two ends of the whole spectrum of our existence, as human beings.

The Root of Addiction

When we are out of touch with our transcendent self, and have forgotten our wholeness, we believe we need to acquire something from the outside in order to be complete. We might attempt to do this through acquiring material possessions or money beyond what we actually need in order to live happily. We might try to do it through relationships, in the hope that another person will complete us. We might use drugs or alcohol, which temporarily give us an experience of expanded consciousness or numb out negative feelings. Because all these things give us only a momentary feeling of wholeness, we tend to chase after them, again and again. We hope their effects will last longer next time. But the more we chase something outside ourselves to find our wholeness, the more we lose touch with our true essence. When we repeatedly go after something "out there" to fill us up, we will feel emptier inside.

All addictive behavior stems from our inability to recognize our inherent wholeness, and the belief that something outside us can return us to a feeling of peace and comfort. It is as though we have our own umbilical cord in our hand, trying to find a place to plug it in, in an attempt to reconnect with ourselves. But the feeling of connection only occurs and remains when we uncover what is buried, within—our true essence. Addiction is so prevalent in our lives these days that we don't even always recognize it for what it is. We typically think of addicts as people who abuse alcohol or drugs. But any repeated compulsive act where we are seeking outside ourselves and that is damaging to our quality of life, is addictive behavior. Even some spiritual or religious practices can become addictions. If they create an unhealthy dependency on somebody or a particular teaching outside of us, they can prevent us from reconnecting with the transcendent self within. Although dependency on an external representation of our transcendent self might be a helpful stage along the way, our ultimate satisfaction only occurs when we experience union with our essence, our being.

The Shadow Self

Our shadow self refers to those elements of ourselves that we have disowned or buried below the surface. Many of us try to keep our shadow-self hidden, not only from others but from our very own selves. Our shadow is a collection of those parts we learned as "bad," and we therefore judge them as unacceptable and unlovable. The shadow self also holds those parts that we believe are too painful to feel, including the unhealed traumas of our past. We often hide emotions like anger, fear, resentment, jealousy, intense pain, deep grief, as well as feelings of greed and aggression in our shadow self. When we refuse to acknowledge these "darker" aspects of ourselves, we live in fear that others will see them, and judge us—just as we judge ourselves. And when we see those same traits in others, we judge and criticize *them*, for displaying the very traits we deem unacceptable in ourselves. In psychological terms, this is known as projection. Quite often, we see and judge in others what we refuse to accept about ourselves, or in many cases even fail to recognize.

As human beings, it is sometimes easier for us to point the finger at another, making *them* wrong, rather than accepting the fact that we are also capable of displaying dark emotions and behaviors. What triggers us in another person is therefore an accurate indication of what we are projecting onto that person, and hiding from ourselves. When we are triggered by somebody or something "out there," it would behoove us to accept it as the gift it truly is. It is a gift because it gives us important insight into a blind spot about ourselves. When we are emotionally triggered by somebody else's behavior, we often shut down and close off, making the other person "wrong" for what triggered us. But we can choose to remain open and accept the gift that has been offered us. When we have the courage to get curious about what we are hiding from ourselves, we are accepting the opportunity to deepen our self-honesty. We are accepting the opportunity to be compassionate with ourselves and to therefore deepen the intimacy of our relationship with ourselves and the world around us.

Integrating the Shadow

Along the journey of finding our wholeness, it is important that we have the courage to face and embrace every aspect of our shadow self, no matter how difficult that might be. We integrate our shadow by first allowing it to be, just as it is, and accepting it. Then we understand it—in the same way we have understanding and compassion for a small, innocent child who is misbehaving but does not know any better. We know that the child deserves our love, no matter what. Until we accept and feel compassion for our shadow self, we remain divided within. And we continue to create conflict without, by making others wrong. And as is often said: "Would you rather be right or happy?"

Taking a clear, honest look at our shadow self may not be easy. It requires humility and a great deal of courage. It does not do us any good to see our shadow and judge it. That is how it became our shadow in the first place. Like a wayward child, the elements of our shadow need our loving attention and our acceptance. Allowing another person—maybe a trusted, nonjudgmental friend or a spiritual counselor or a therapist—to witness those parts of ourselves that we have kept carefully hidden, can be an important step in our process of healing and integration. And, integration always precedes transformation.

After acknowledging these darker aspects of ourselves, we come to see that they are not now, and never were the truth of who we are. They are the by-product of *forgetting* our true identity. They are the result of the emotional wounding we experienced at the hand of others—as a result of *their forgetting* their true identity. Our shadow exists because we have believed in the story of our separation from the rest of life. Believing in separation creates fear-based thinking and action. Our true self has the capacity to compassionately witness our shadow and to see it for what it is. The simple act of shining the light of loving awareness on our shadow enables us to integrate it, and allows us to recognize our true nature.

Spiritual Bypass

Sometimes we try to avoid or sidetrack dealing with the difficult aspects of human life by using spiritual concepts and practices to "spiritually bypass" the things we do not want to face. We *pretend* that we do not feel angry, resentful, or hurt by somebody else's words or actions. We believe that it is "not spiritual" to feel these emotions. Possibly, on a subconscious level, we would rather not deal with them, or we are afraid to look. Perhaps from another level of consciousness we would not have the same emotional reactions, however, it is important to be honest with ourselves about where we are. Allowing ourselves to compassionately practice present moment awareness is a tool we can use for walking *through* these experiences rather than bypassing them.

Self-Forgiveness

Self-forgiveness is reclaiming our innocence. It means letting go of our ideas about how we thought we "should" have done things differently. We let go of the belief that we "should" have known what we didn't know then. We let go of the story that we "should" have been something we were not then, or that we "should" have acted in a way that we were not capable of at that time. Forgiveness—whether of ourselves or of another—is a choice. It might take time to finally arrive at the place where we recognize our true innocence. It might take time to recognize the innocence of others, no matter what their apparent injustice. This quote by Archbishop Desmond Tutu says it well: "*To forgive is the highest form of self-interest. I need to forgive so that my anger and resentment and lust for revenge don't corrode my own being.*"

We are 100 percent accountable for our lives. But if our life does not look the way we think we want it to, it can be easy to fall into the trap of making ourselves "wrong." Self-criticism is not the same as self-responsibility or self-accountability. Self-criticism is never helpful. We understand that our lives are a reflection of our very own consciousness and that our thoughts create our daily experiences. However, when something happens that we don't want—an illness for example—this is not a reason to make ourselves wrong. Blaming ourselves for getting sick is what is sometimes referred to as metaphysical malpractice. When we hear the voice of the inner critic, we can thank it for sharing (without judging it for judging) and decide not to take it seriously. After all, it is the voice of our limited ego, rather than the voice of our true essence. We can use these moments as an entry point to deepen our compassion for ourselves instead, by sending love and support, in the form of constructive self-talk. Just as we would give support and encouragement to a small child who needed it in order to grow and develop.

Moving Beyond Limitation

In the 1960s, a rare white Bengal tiger arrived at the National Zoo in Washington, D.C. The tiger, named Mohini, was a special gift to President Eisenhower and the people of America from the government of India. Mohini was placed in a temporary 12 x 12–foot cage, while the zoo discussed plans to build her a magnificent enclosure. The enclosure was to resemble her natural habitat, with lush forests, rolling hills, and everything a tiger could possibly need or want. During the construction period, Mohini paced around her cramped cage, in a figure-8 pattern, day after day. Unexpected delays in building the new habitat turned months into years, as the young tiger continued to pace around her small cage.

Finally, Mohini's new, spacious enclosure was completed and a large crowd gathered to witness the big event. At long last, she would be able to experience her freedom. To the crowd's great surprise, however, on entering her new home, Mohini headed straight to the far corner and started pacing around in the same figure-8 pattern, just as she had been forced to do for several years. Sadly, she spent the rest of her life in the small far corner of her enclosure, moving in the same figure-8, 12 x 12 pattern, completely oblivious to the paradise surrounding her.

This story illustrates what happens when we allow our earlier programming to dictate the limits of our awareness and of our experience of life. My question to you is: What is *your* self-imposed, 12 x 12, figure-8 pattern? How are you living within the confines of an inherited belief system that still appears to be "real" for you? The truth is that you have the capacity to experience infinite freedom from within. You live in an infinitely abundant universe. It is only the limitations of your thinking, and the stories you tell yourself, that keep you tightly contained in a life that might feel smaller than you would like it to be.

Expanding Consciousness

A helpful image of expanding consciousness, I learned from my good friend and teacher Rev. Maureene Bass. Imagine lots of dots drawn on a piece of paper. If you draw a circle enclosing 8 dots or so, this circle represents a particular level of consciousness. If you expand the circle, and draw a larger one containing 12 dots, this represents a consciousness that has expanded. For example, your consciousness might have expanded after a spiritual study or a life experience that caused you to grow your awareness in a certain way. As you continue to grow spiritually, your consciousness continues to expand, and the circle continues to grow larger, enclosing more and more dots. And it continues, ad infinitum.

I invite you to take a look at the places where your understanding, your *human* consciousness, feels limited and restricted. Any limitation that you are currently experiencing is not ultimately "real." It's only as real as the 12x12 limitation Mohini the tiger experienced when transferred to a larger enclosure. Mohini didn't have the self-awareness to deconstruct her limited inner reality. But as a human, you have the ability to take your self-imposed limitations and see them for what they are—illusions based on past experience. By letting them go, your consciousness naturally expands to encompass a greater reality.

Awakening Happens Now

Waking up to who you truly are is something that can only possibly happen in this present moment. The mind thinks of awakening as a process and tells itself, "I'm not there yet." It imagines what it will be like, at some future time, when it arrives. But that is affirming "I'm not awake now." It is closing the door on the possibility of experiencing the truth of who and what you are, in this moment. In every moment, you have full access to your essential self, to the truth of who you are. You could say that this moment now is the most enlightened you'll ever be. What do you choose to do with that? In other words, this is not a dress rehearsal. This moment holds all the potential you need to know the truth of who you are and what you are capable of experiencing in the outer realm.

Awakening or enlightenment is simply recognition of the truth. There is nothing to figure out. It is being fully present, in this moment, in the body, as a spiritual experience. It is accepting the parts that feel glorious, happy, and connected *and* those parts that feel shut down, tight, or closed off. You do not have to do anything with what you notice, but rather fully accept and experience it, just as it is and recognize that there is an ultimate reality much greater than your mind can comprehend.

The Value of Spiritual Community

One of the greatest gifts of being part of a spiritual community is the support system of people who know and believe in the truth of who and what they really are, at the level of essence. A group of people who are committed to seeing us beyond our self-imposed limitations is of tremendous value. Spiritual friends and community remind us, when we seemingly forget, of our wholeness and spiritual perfection. When we are caught up in the illusion of our self-limiting stories and forget our true identity—as love, light, and truth—we can be reminded, by those who *see us* as love, light, and truth. This is the highest purpose of community.

There are those who seek out spiritual community in the hope that others will fix them or do their personal work for them. But we are the only ones who can do our own inner work. Nobody outside of us can fix us, no matter how much they might want to. (And remember, we are not broken) But they can support us as we take steps on our inner journey, and to reflect back to us the progress we are making.

At Awakened Living (Our spiritual community in San Francisco), we offer our full support to those seeking to know the truth of who they are. Our intention is to provide a forum for like-minded people from diverse backgrounds to come together. We celebrate each other and see the truth of who we are; prefect aspects of the divine. Our commitment is to see ourselves and each other as inherently whole and perfect. If at times we lose touch with our wholeness, and find ourselves acting from our old conditioning, that is OK. Community members can hold a mirror up to us, inviting us to look within. They can encourage us to inquire whether there is a piece of our metaphoric 12 X 12 cage that is causing us to move in a habitual figure-8 pattern. We might discover an unresolved hurt from the past. We might find a deeply ingrained belief that keeps us focused on 10 dots when there are 10 billion. A loving, supportive community can help us see through our inner illusions and help to set us free.

The deepest surrender we will ever make is to know we are one with spirit. Ultimate freedom comes from experiencing ourselves as we truly are—a perfect expression of the one.

Chapter Four

CONSCIOUS EVOLUTION

"You can't talk about the ocean with a frog who lives in a well. He is bounded by the space he inhabits. You can't talk about ice with an insect who was born in June. He is bounded by a single season. You can't talk about the Tao with a person who thinks he knows something. He is bounded by his own beliefs. The Tao is vast and fathomless. You can understand only by stepping beyond the limits of yourself."

— *Excerpt from* The Second Book of the Tao, *by Stephen Mitchell*

Levels of Consciousness

As I journey through my life, I have noticed that when I arrive at a place I have strived to be, the question "Now what?" often arises in my mind. Once I have accomplished what I thought I wanted (internally or externally), I find myself at another new beginning. I am ready to expand my level of understanding from the one I previously held. Looking back, I can identify four levels of understanding, or levels of human consciousness, which I offer here as a framework of reference. (I am referring to human consciousness in this conversation, which is different than ultimate, eternal, and changeless Consciousness.) I have named these levels: Martyr,

Magical, Metaphysical, and Mystical. Although there is a forward progression in evolving from one level to the next, the movement is not entirely linear. Even though I may have attained a higher level of awareness, I can find myself back at a lower one in an instant when something happens that triggers an old reactive pattern. Most of us intermittently slip into one level or another, but in my experience, we are each *primarily* operating from one of these following levels. These levels get played out at both the micro and the macro levels.

Level 1: Martyr State of Consciousness

"Things happen to me."

This level is outer focused and seeks answers and solutions from others. At this level, we live in a paradigm where we believe that "things happen *to us*." We frequently feel powerless over our circumstances and other people's behavior. We have no control over our reactions to what happens in our lives. In this "reality," it appears as though there are powerful external forces that sometimes work against us and our will. This level could also be described as "victim consciousness." We experience these external forces as circumstances—people (especially authority figures), the government, God, or life in general. At this level, we believe that in order to increase our happiness, we need to manipulate and change our outer world in order to get our needs and desires met. We may say things like, "If only *they* would change or behave differently..." or "If only I could get what I want (usually the 'right' job, partner, home, car, etc.) *then* I'd be happy." We feel dependent on externals for our sense of fulfillment and well-being.

If we live in this "reality" (which is rooted in a belief in separation), our idea of power is that of *power over* other people and things. We believe others wield power over us. If we believe in a higher power, it takes the form of an external, authoritarian, judging, punishing (or rewarding) God. We do our best to obey God's will, so that He (At this level, God is often perceived as a male figure) will treat us right. And if we do not get what we want in life, we say that we are not living up to God's expectations of us. We think we are doing something wrong. Many of the world's religions and governments operate at this level. They make clear-cut distinctions of what is "right or wrong" and what is "good or bad." In this paradigm, enemies seem very real. We believe that if people would follow the rules, and do the "right thing," then society would function smoothly and peacefully. This is an animalistic consciousness. It is most often motivated by fear, and the primary identity is with the physical body. Much of the world is still operating at this level of consciousness. It is evidenced by war, famine, and the drive for power and dominance that riddle society. In many circles, this is considered to be quite normal. A look at the growing prison population in America, and the need to punish, demonstrates how many of us are rooted in this consciousness.

Powerlessness and Addiction

Living at the martyr level of black-and-white thinking, it is easy to fall into a state of hopelessness or depression when we are not able to get what we want in life. Temporary relief from feelings of powerlessness is often found in some form of addictive behavior. The addiction can be to alcohol, drugs, love, sex, shopping, food, television, technology, work, or something else. Those who live at the extreme end of this level have often experienced some form of childhood trauma or abuse. They often carry unresolved issues within themselves. Being a victim of childhood abuse—of whatever degree—can lead a person to conclude, at a young age, that something is wrong with them and the world and that it is not possible to change their circumstances later in life. Some people remain in the victim state of consciousness for their entire life. I want to be clear; I am not saying that, as children, there are not "victims" of heinous acts, but it is our responsibility as adults to examine our current world view and do the inner work necessary to release past traumas and move to another way of being, if we want to live a happy and connected life.

The majority of humanity operates—to a greater or lesser degree—at the martyr level. News headlines portray stories of conflict and power-play, whether it is between individuals or nations. For many, living at the martyr level is somewhat acceptable, if their basic needs are being met. That is until something occurs that causes them to question the world in which they live. It might be a major loss, an illness, or some other traumatic event. Pain is what often wakes people up from this level of awareness. It causes them to inquire whether there might be another way of living. The frustration of unsuccessfully trying to manipulate the external world to their satisfaction can also drive them to seek answers on a deeper level.

The Causal Point of Change

Sometimes, an unexpected glimpse into the spiritual realm or a "peak experience" can cause us to remember that there is more to existence than our physical senses would have us believe. We might discover that another, expanded state of being is possible. We may have had a brief glimpse of one, and we feel a sense of urgency about living in it. But for most of us, an inner journey needs to be embarked upon before we find ourselves at the next level, in a sustained, stabilized way. Our journey will probably entail facing and healing some difficult emotional realities in the form of hurts and traumas from our past.

In order to relieve ourselves of these invisible burdens we carry, we need to fully own our past. Only then can we release the unhealed hurts that we are still carrying. As much as we might want to avoid the discomfort of this emotional healing work, it is necessary to face these difficult inner places. We need to awaken to our pain, in order that we can fully awaken to our joy. My personal experience, including years of working with clients in addiction treatment centers, has taught me that the spiritual journey involves learning to *be with* our discomfort. We cannot avoid it if we want to be free. We cannot possibly rise to the heights of our joy unless we are willing to also experience, and make friends with, the depths of our pain.

Level 2: Magical Thinking Consciousness

"I make things happen."

This level is primarily outer-focused and result oriented. It is usually a welcome relief to discover that by taking greater ownership of our thoughts, and by directing them in focused ways, we can positively affect the events and outcomes in our lives. In this next level of consciousness, which I call magical thinking, we realize that causative power is not only outside us, but also within. By changing our thinking we begin to control our experiences and understand that we can effect change in areas of our lives where we formerly felt powerless. It feels like magic. In order to live effectively in this reality, we do not blame others for our unwanted circumstances and feelings. We are willing to take 100 percent responsibility for both our inner and outer lives and recognize we are responsible for causing them.

Many New Thought teachings operate at this level. They teach us how to use positive affirmations and thought awareness in order to manifest the lives we want to live. In this reality, in order to increase our happiness, we ask ourselves: "What do I want, and how can I create it?" The majority of obstacles we encounter are those from within. They often come from our self-doubt or feelings of undeservedness. We address those issues and change our focus to a new way of *thinking*. We work on our abundance issues. We affirm things like: "I love money and money loves me," or "I'm a money-magnet." We learn techniques to manipulate the world to suit our desires. We think we have total control over our lives and that the world will rearrange itself to bring us what we want. That is as long as we focus on the "right" or affirmative thoughts.

At the magical thinking level, we might understand the important truth that quantum physics has revealed to us in recent years. The new thinking is that, at an energy level, everything is interconnected. Knowing this we can grasp the concept that we have the power within us to shift and control our external reality. However, a possible trap is that we may be still living in an egocentric place. That means that our choices and desires arise from our separate ego self, rather than from a deeper level of connection with others and with the whole of life.

At this level, we are primarily identified with the mind. We most likely still have some attachments to outcomes and are dependent on filling our inner void with things from the outside in order to be happy. In my own life, I used mind awareness techniques and affirmations to successfully build the life of my dreams. I acquired all that I wanted on a material level. My experience, however, was that once I had achieved my outer goals, I discovered that I still had an inner yearning for something more. Another "Now what?" moment presented itself, which led me to the level of consciousness that I call Metaphysical.

Level 3: Metaphysical Consciousness

"Things happen through me/I let things happen."

This level is inner focused and answers are internal. In order to enter into this next level of consciousness, we discover the willingness to relinquish our sense of control, and we allow life to happen *through us*. In this reality, we understand that we are part of a larger, interconnected whole and that our individual purpose is tied up with the purpose of that whole. We are willing to trust a higher intelligence to guide and inform us about our place in the world. We choose to be used by divine intelligence in a way that serves the well-being of humanity. We want to find our rightful role in the larger scheme of things, and we trust in a divine order. Even though we cannot personally see the bigger picture from our ego's narrow perspective, we believe that our fulfillment is derived from our willingness to cooperate with a higher intelligence that sees the broader view. We trust in the guidance of the still, small voice within, more so than the limited perspective of the logical mind.

At this level, we choose to surrender to a higher power, but not in the subservient, codependent way that we did at the martyr level. At that level, our relationship to a higher power was comparable to a child's relationship to a dysfunctional parent. We were afraid that if we made a "wrong" move, we would be punished. We were intent on pleasing the all-powerful father figure, and *his will* took priority over our personal will. At the metaphysical level, the metaphor is one of a trusting, loving partnership between equals. We trust that source wants the best for us. It is supporting us in getting our needs met and in succeeding in our goals. Having surrendered to this higher will, we have aligned our personal desires with those of the whole. We're therefore able to let go and relax, trusting that life will take care of us. We are committed to doing our part to serve life, knowing that this will bring us the ultimate satisfaction.

At the metaphysical level we are no longer completely identified with our minds. We have learned to pay attention to the inner knowing of our intuition. We understand that our intuition arises from a place of connectedness to the whole, and is therefore the mouthpiece of higher intelligence. We experience our connection with others and with life through the heart. Our primary identification is with the heart. We know that in order to function at our best, we need to use our whole brain, rather than being overly dependent on either left or right brain thinking. In this reality, we are aware of our "personal desires," but we don't necessarily see them as personal any more. We realize that, as a unique strand in the web of life, our desires are delivered to us from within. Life prompts us to serve its higher purpose. We have learned that it is therefore our responsibility to honor what is true for us. We don't deny our truth out of fear that it will not match somebody else's truth, or their expectation of us. Living authentically, to the best of our ability, is how we serve life.

Self-Love

Living at the metaphysical level requires that we learn to love ourselves. We love ourselves in all the ways we have wanted and expected others to love us. We forgive ourselves for whatever wrongs we believe we committed. Because of this, we feel loved and cared for from within. We are no longer dependent on external circumstances or others to make us feel complete. We are plugged into our inner source of happiness. We can therefore enjoy the movement of life as it flows through us, no matter what might be happening. We no longer feel the need to use force in order to get what we want. We understand that when we are aligned with our purpose (which is connected to the whole), things naturally fall into place. We have no need for stress or worry. We trust that life is taking care of the details. Rather than believing that we are creating our own reality, we realize that life has already created an abundant world. We can simply allow ourselves to be guided to our highest and best, which already exists. We just need to open our eyes to it, and be willing to receive.

Level 4: Mystical Consciousness

"Things happen *as me*."

Beyond the metaphysical level is mystical consciousness. This level is an inner-focused consciousness where no outer answers are needed. At this level, we call off the search and rest in the truth that has always been. From here, there is no longer any real distinction between ourselves and the world around us. Neither is there any separation between us and spirit. From this place we understand—both intellectually and experientially—that all is one. We therefore are not capable of doing anything separate from the energy that creates and moves everything in this world. This energy moves our bodies, speaks our words, and thinks our thoughts. In this reality, we are the eyes, ears, hands, and feet of divine love. We perceive that life is happening *as us*. Our primary identity is with spirit. We understand that everything that is occurring is a perfect expression of source energy. We know that whatever another says or does—it is a perfect expression of the divine. It is God in action. In this reality, there is no longer any distinction between "right and wrong," or "good and bad." There is no such thing as an enemy. There is only the continuously unfolding, moment-to-moment expression of life, which arises from one source. There is just *what is*, and it is all sacred.

When we find ourselves at this mystical level, there is no longer any seeking for anything other than what we are presently experiencing. This moment is enough. We no longer seek peace, but rather we *are* peace. We no longer seek love, because we know ourselves to *be* love. We realize that *we are what we've been seeking*. There is an awareness of the unchanging, eternal presence that witnesses this moment. There is total acceptance of what is happening in this ever-changing moment. In this state, there is nothing to *do*. There is nothing to hold on to. There is nothing to acquire. No answers. No questions.

Trusting the Process

As I have mentioned, moving through these stages is not always a linear process. My experience is that at one moment we can be feeling perfectly surrendered, trusting that all is exactly as it should be, and the next, we might be feeling anxiety over an outcome that matters to us. Or, we might notice judgmental thoughts arising in our minds. We might have a negative reaction to what someone says to us, and suddenly we are back in a mind-set in which we feel powerless over the circumstances. We might feel the need to exert some control, or we might want to let somebody know that they are "wrong," and we are "right." The difference is that we no longer need to take our thoughts seriously. We can choose what we do with them. We have the clarity to see our old reactive mechanism for what it is. We understand that it no longer serves us. We are free to choose a different internal response than in the past. We can return to a more loving, heart-centered perspective within seconds, rather than hours, days, or weeks.

Another example is that we might feel like the victim of someone's verbal or physical attack. We can instantaneously understand (in seconds or minutes) their words or actions are a product of their own level of consciousness. And we find compassion for them. We also no longer feel the need to judge ourselves when we momentarily find ourselves thinking, speaking, or acting from a lower level of consciousness. As soon as we become aware of it, we experience compassion for ourselves. And we can choose to let it go. Because we are no longer identified with our thoughts, we can observe them and release the ones that are not useful. This is how we gently return to a deeper understanding and awareness of life.

The God Idea

Throughout history, and on our planet now, the idea of a God or a Creator is reflected based on one's level of consciousness. We, as humans, have created the "God idea" in our image built on our individual and collective levels of awareness.

Level 1: Martyr—God as Force or Savior

In this consciousness, God, Goddess, or Gods are a powerful outside force and need to be feared, or it/they are seen as a savior. In early cultures, if natural disasters occurred, people prayed to the gods of nature and assumed they had done something out of alignment with the will of the gods. At this level of awareness, God can also be seen as an outside force that can save us or forgive us for our sins. Some people say, "God spared our house in the tornado because we prayed to Him." This is a perfect example of the martyr level of consciousness. Although, there have been individuals and small groups of people living at other levels throughout time, most of human history has lived and still lives at this level of awareness.

Level 2: Magical—God as Law

In the late 19th century, the New Thought movement was born and a profound new consciousness emerged. The movement might be seen as a blending of science and religion. A small but powerful group of people began to discover that human minds produce external reality. This idea was revolutionary. It was understood that thoughts are matter and, as such, create material reality and affect the physical plane. God became impersonal principle. In many ways, the movement is seen as us merging with God Mind.

Level 3: Metaphysical—God as Loving

This level is where much of the New Age exists. The idea of "God" or "Universe" as a loving and gentle power dominates this consciousness. The conversation at this level is inner connectedness, peace, and harmony. People use crystals, tarot cards, runes, and the like as tools to access a divine plan. They use affirmations as a way to lift themselves to a more loving existence. This is classically represented by the hippie movement in the 1960s. At this level, people believe God lives within us, usually seen as living in our hearts.

Level 4: Mystical—God as Love

At this level, God, or the "God idea," is simply everything. Themes of oneness, perfection, and bliss are associated with this level of awareness. God not only lives in you, but *is* you. At this level, you might not use the word God, but refer to Energy, Consciousness, or Light as the ultimate power. You are no longer separate in *any way*. God as love is the only true reality. You surrender to an internal power. You are guided by inner-knowing and meditation, not prayer, which becomes the way to access this inner voice. There is currently an entire movement sweeping the planet coming into alignment with this greater reality.

Recognizing Your Level

This framework has many practical applications. It can be a tool for raising awareness and living a more peaceful and connected life. One way to begin is to question the level at which you are operating, by taking simple real life situations and exploring where you are "living." Here is one such example: Imagine that you are having a discussion with a friend about a chair. You might see the chair as blue and she sees it as green. Here are examples of what you might say from different levels:

> 1st level: "Let me tell you why I know the chair is blue!!!"
> 2nd level: "I know it is blue, but I don't need to prove it to you."
> 3rd level: "I understand that you see it as green. It is possible it is both, depending on perspective."
> 4th level: "It literally does not matter to me what the color is." Nothing needs to be said at all.

Another framework points out how you view your relationship between human and spirit. You've probably heard it said that you're not a human being having a spiritual experience but you are a spiritual being having a human experience. The following are four ways of viewing life, which correspond with the four levels of consciousness described.

> 1st level: Human beings having a human experience.
> 2nd level: Human beings have a spiritual experience.
> 3rd level: Spiritual beings have a human experience.
> 4th level: Spiritual beings have a spiritual experience.

Tools for Spiritual Unfolding

What causes us to move up through these levels of consciousness? Consciousness itself. The more awareness we have, the greater our ability to see where we are internally residing. And in the seeing, we transform. There is no foolproof series of steps that, if taken, will ensure deliverance into unity consciousness. We can, however, use whatever transformational tools we have, when we need them, which keep us moving in an evolutionary direction. Meditation is one of the most powerful tools we can utilize. Meditation increases our conscious awareness because it takes us out of our limited, mentally focused reality. It enables us to step back and observe our thoughts objectively. We see them for what they are. Meditation enables us to go beyond our thinking mind. We can experience a freedom that we cannot possibly know while we are confined within the reality of our thoughts. Meditation aligns us with higher intelligence and our inner guidance.

Another powerful tool is identifying and questioning our thoughts. With inquiry, we discover that all our suffering arises from our thinking, rather than from what is happening. The Work of Byron Katie is a process that provides us with a simple, effective tool to undo and release the beliefs that cause our suffering.

I believe that spending time around others who share our intention of raising consciousness is an important support for our awakening. Being with spiritual community on a regular basis can ensure our advancement on the path of spiritual awakening. Community can provide consistent, reliable nurturing for our spiritual unfolding.

Sane or Insane?

The levels of consciousness I have described might appear to be nonsensical or even insane. You may be experiencing a reaction or resistance to the discussion of these levels. If you feel acivated, it might point to the level in which you are currently operating. For example, if the writing about the magical level triggered you or caused you to feel uncomfortable, it might be that you are presently operating from that level, or possibly the previous level.

As previously stated, the majority of humanity is currently functioning from the martyr level. If you decide to work on raising your consciousness, you might well be judged by some others as "insane." Becoming saner can feel odd. That is until you are firmly grounded in the new consciousness and have come to trust it. From my perspective, the culture in which we currently live can be viewed as insane. Is it sane to celebrate competition, perpetuate violence, and participate in abuse of varying types? This, to me, is quite insane. What is accepted in the collective would be diagnosed and treated as a mental illness in the individual. America could easily be viewed as having narcissistic, paranoid, and attention deficit disorders, to name a few. We are also taught not to trust what we authentically feel. Society sometimes insists that there is something "wrong" with people who are sensitive to their emotions, or people who feel deeply. We have a medical system that often advises us to medicate people rather than address their underlying issues. The root cause is a spiritual malady. The answer is spiritual in nature, and has nothing to do with the "problem."

Our feelings are important indicators of what is happening within us. They provide valuable signposts along our life-path. A culture that dismisses the higher intelligence of intuition, because its messages do not come through the more acceptable channel of logical thinking, is not a very developed culture. And a culture that pits one religion against another, one race against another and one sexual orientation against another is not an emotionally healthy one. Societies that resort to physical violence and abuse, in an attempt to dominate and control, are in my mind intrinsically insane. More accurately, a culture that does not understand or value the intelligence of feeling and intuition is spiritually and emotionally immature. A society that is not able to peacefully accept different viewpoints and belief systems has some important growing to do.

A Call to Action

It is absolutely imperative that we evolve and grow in consciousness at this time in our evolution. Not only does the survival of the planet require this, but we must make this shift if we are to find true happiness and peace. It is up to each of us to do the inner work necessary to fully engage the new paradigm.

We are at a unique time in history where lasting peace can prevail because enough of us have the awareness to create a world filled with love and harmony. However, what is required now is a new kind of action. It is an inner action. We must each become accountable for our own conscious evolution and make the internal changes required to manifest a world that works for all. It starts with a decision.

Chapter Five

HEAVEN ON EARTH

"The Great Way is not difficult for those who are unattached to their preferences. Let go of longing and aversion and everything will be perfectly clear. When you cling to a hair-breadth of distinction, heaven and earth are set apart. If you want to realize the Truth, don't be for or against. The struggle between good and evil is the primary disease of our mind. Not grasping the deeper meaning, you just trouble your mind's serenity. As vast as infinite space, it is perfect and lacks nothing. But because you select and reject, you cannot perceive its true nature. Be at peace with the oneness of things, and all errors will disappear by themselves."

— *Excerpt from* The Mind of Absolute Trust, *by Seng Ts'an*

Collective Influence

A few years ago, my nephew, who was eight years old at the time, and I were walking down the street, when we came across a large hole next to the road. On seeing the hole, my nephew said, "Uncle TJ, be careful. Don't step there, you might fall into hell!" He said this as though he absolutely believed it were true. Given that he was brought up by nonreligious parents, and without any religious education at school, I was somewhat surprised that he believed such an idea. I took the opportunity to inquire some more about what he believed. He continued, "Well, if you're good, you go to heaven. And if you're bad, you go to hell." It was amazing to me that, even without any formal religious education, he firmly believed in this reality.

Changing Paradigms

There are certain paradigms of thinking that exist within our collective consciousness. They powerfully shape our inner world. Many of us never take the time to examine these frameworks of thinking more closely. My invitation to you is to acknowledge that you have access to an inner source of knowing, which is beyond any learned concepts. This intuitive knowing is not arrived at through thinking or learning, but rather by tuning into the intelligence of the heart. The paradigm shift that human consciousness is currently undergoing is very much about shifting from mind-based knowing to heart-based, intuitive being.

If you were to ask people who lived 100 years ago—in the year 1915—what changes would happen over the next 100 years, it would have been impossible for them to anticipate the transformations that were to occur. Looking back, we can see that it was beyond the capacity of their imaginations to envision the world in which we live today. The highly sophisticated technology that we now use on a daily basis and take for granted would have been unthinkable to people at the beginning of the 20th century. And, although nobody can predict what life will look like in 100 years, I have a strong sense that the next major transformation will be in the realm of spiritual consciousness.

Many spiritual leaders and great thinkers of our time agree that a new consciousness is being born within humanity. It is clear that we are currently at a turning point where the old consciousness has been outgrown and can now be released. We can already see that many old structures on the planet are in the process of crumbling in order to make way for the birth of the new. Financial markets, political systems, religions, and even countries are undergoing profound instability. While the visible change is being reflected in the outer world, I foresee more of an inner transformation happening in the near future. The new technologies, which allow us to be easily connected with each other, have been an important preparation for the inner transformation that is to come. The next step is an upgrade of our "inner technology." This involves a leap from mind-based intelligence (which is rooted in the idea of separation) to heart-based being (which is rooted in oneness). At the level of the heart, human beings are already intrinsically linked to each other.

The Old Paradigm

The old paradigm is one in which logical thinking was considered to be the highest form of intelligence. As discussed in the previous chapter, the New Thought movement was one in which the mind was recognized as the source of all creation. This movement ushered in the new consciousness of the 20th Century. The foundation of this movement was the idea that infinite intelligence or God is omniscient—everywhere, and in everything, including human beings. This meant that all human beings had personal and equal access to infinite intelligence, through their individual minds. It was understood that we each have a separate mind, which is connected to, or one with infinite mind, or God Mind. Each individual mind is endowed with the same qualities as infinite mind. Human beings are therefore divine beings, all possessing equal ability to use the creative capacity of divine mind. They can use the positive force for good, and for healing.

In the late 1800s, when the New Thought movement was born, the thinking was that every human being has access to—or possesses—infinite creative power. This was a huge paradigm shift. At that time, the old framework of understanding was that divine creative power was exclusively in the hands of an external God. This old way of thinking stated that, as human beings, we were subordinate to a powerful, superior God. It was believed that we needed to surrender our will to this external patriarchal God being. (Reflecting the martyr level of consciousness as described in the previous chapter) This new paradigm put creative power in our own hands. It said we are each responsible for what we experience. It allowed each of us to change the circumstances of our lives by drawing on and using this inwardly accessed creative power. This was an absolutely revolutionary idea at the time.

Ernest Holmes's classic book, *The Science of Mind*, was influential in reorienting our understanding of our place in the world. It explained how, by changing our thinking, we could change the outcomes we experienced in our daily lives. It gave us the science that proved that we are not victims of our circumstances. We are actually powerfully creative beings. New Thought churches base their teachings on these truths. (Which reflect what I call the magical thinking level) New Thought churches today include Unity Church, the Church of Divine Science, and Centers for Spiritual Living (previously known as the United Church of Religious Science), to name a few.

Although the New Thought movement was—and still is—important in the evolution of our spiritual understanding, it only takes us so far. It is empowering to know that our minds are one with the creative source energy that shapes our daily experiences. It is significant that we can work with that energy in order to manifest our personal desires. However, this level of understanding is not the highest truth. Many of the New Thought traditions are themselves evolving in consciousness and some are even experiencing "growing pains." Some factions within the movements want to stay "true" to the original teachings of the founders. Other members are ready to embrace and celebrate the emergence of the new consciousness.

There are people who consider the New Thought teachings to be "selfish." They judge them as being only about "me and my own desires." However, this stage of understanding is an important one in developing a distinct and autonomous sense of self, spiritually speaking. Without this developmental phase, we would remain at the level of childish, codependent, and fearful patterns of thinking and behaving. By developing our own spiritual autonomy, we mature into spiritual adults. We need to believe we have the inner resources to stand on our own two feet and take care of our own needs. We can achieve our personal desires and dreams. Otherwise we remain as spiritual children, feeling like victims of an external power that only exists in our imagination.

As unique, autonomous selves, we are all equal. When we trust in our inherent creative capacity to get our needs met, we can release our urgency to compete with others. When we believe we can draw on our internal, creative resources, we feel safe enough to release our fears of lack and limited resources. We no longer need to fight with others over them. When we trust in the power of our infinite creative capacity, we lose the need to exert our power over others. Our fulfillment is no longer dependent on anything or anyone outside of us.

A large portion of human consciousness is now shifting or has shifted to the next level of understanding. I call this the metaphysical level. At this level, we learn that it is safe for us to relax and let go of the need to control our lives. We come to trust that life itself is taking care of us, moment to moment. We realize that we can just relax and allow life to flow *through* us. We understand that the details of our lives will be taken care of, by the inherent intelligence of life itself. We don't have to figure it all out.

As we move forward in developing our understanding, we don't abandon what we learned at previous levels. Rather, we incorporate it into the greater truth that is now unfolding for us. In this way, we continue to expand our consciousness. We have learned to use the creative power of our minds to improve our lives. We realize the value of this skill, not only for ourselves, but also to help others in improving their circumstances. And by joining forces with others, we can become powerfully influential on a larger scale, for the betterment of humankind.

Hell on Earth

You could say that hell consciousness is being identified with a mind that divides and separates, one that uses labels such as "right and wrong," or "good and bad." A mind that judges and blames, and believes its own fearful thoughts—with no way out—is a form of hell. When we identify only with our mind—which is not capable of comprehending our innate oneness with each other—we fail to experience heaven on earth. Minds inherently believe that they are separate. They are not equipped to comprehend paradox. But spiritual truth is paradoxical. It is a paradox that, as human beings, we seem to be both separate *and* one with each other. We therefore need to go beyond the capacity of the thinking mind in order to know and experience the reality of oneness.

The mind, believing it is separate, constantly generates stories that there is something to fear. It does this to confirm and justify its belief in its own separateness. But a mind that believes it must defend itself against potential harm can never truly know peace. When we believe everything our mind tells us, and make it our highest form of knowing, we inevitably suffer. Unfortunately we also believe the source of our suffering is outside of us. To not have a means of escaping the mechanisms of our mind is comparable to living in hell, with no way out. To be identified only with our thinking minds is to be trapped in a place where we can never know our oneness with life.

Only by disidentifying with our thinking mind can we make the shift to a new level of consciousness. When we do, we open ourselves to receive information from a larger, all-inclusive field of knowing. Our intuition, or heart-intelligence, is a mode of knowing that taps into a more expansive web of information. Our heart-intelligence uses a circuitry that connects us to the whole of life. When we listen to, trust, and act on our intuition, our lives can shift and transform in miraculous ways. It is as if unseen forces are pulling the strings and influencing the unfolding of the daily events of our lives. We can live in a world of connectivity, which is readily available to all, once we choose to tap into our intuitive knowing. This will open the doorway to a new way of being in the world.

Recognizing Illusion

Although the planetary shifting of consciousness is already underway, and continuing to gather momentum, the question might arise as to whether there is something we can do in order to help it along. What can we do when we find ourselves suffering in some way, and living in a hellish state of mind? What if we are feeling separate from the rest of life, or in a state of fear and anxiety about our future? What if we have a profound spiritual experience, a clear knowing, of our innate oneness with source? And then, a moment later, through no seeming action of our own, we find ourselves back in the old consciousness, wondering why the bliss did not stay with us. How do we help transform the unhappy world—personally or globally—which we find ourselves living in?

Although we might believe we need to *do* something, the transformation that is currently happening is in *consciousness*. It's all a matter of shifting our perspective. Peace, clarity, and enlightenment are always available to us, from within. If we attempt to change things on the outside, without also addressing what is going on within, then we're just "rearranging the deckchairs on the Titanic," as the saying goes.

In his book *A New Earth*, Eckhart Tolle says, "*The good news is that if you recognize illusion as illusion, it dissolves. The recognition of illusion is also its ending. Its survival depends upon you mistaking it for reality. In seeing who you are not, the reality of who you are emerges by itself.*" So, the shift is less about *doing* and more about choosing a new way of *being*. It is about recognizing how we are creating the illusions in our life—because we are looking through the lens of our mind, disconnected from the larger, truer understanding of our heart. In fact, whenever we view anyone or any situation as less than pure love, light, or source—we are creating an illusion. We believe what our mind is telling us, rather than what our heart knows.

Albert Einstein said it like this: "*A human being is a part of the whole....He experiences himself, his thoughts and feelings as something separated from the rest, a kind of optical delusion of his consciousness. This delusion is a kind of prison for us....Our task must be to free ourselves from this prison by widening our circle of compassion to embrace all living creatures and the whole of nature.*" Einstein's wisdom points to the necessity of breaking out of the prison of our individual mind and knowing ourselves as something vastly greater than our human mind is capable of comprehending.

Crumbling Structures

We do not need to abandon the mind's intelligence—it is, after all, our trusted servant. But we do need to understand its proper role. The mind's highest purpose is to serve love. Not the other way around. The intuitive mind does not use man-made structures—beliefs and opinions—for knowing. As we shift into new consciousness, we realize that the old structures, which no longer support the new, must crumble. This relates to both external and internal structures. Any ideas, beliefs, or opinions, which no longer support the new consciousness, will need to give way in order to make way for the new.

As we find ourselves making these inner shifts in perspective, we will most likely experience changes in our external circumstances too. In my own experience of transforming consciousness, there was a time when my life started falling apart. The external structures I had worked so hard to create—job, home, relationships—started to crumble. Although it was an extremely difficult period of my life, I now see it was a gift. It was an enormous blessing that my old life fell apart, for it allowed my new life to take shape. The incredibly fulfilling life I now live could never have emerged if my old life had not disintegrated.

Having our external world crumble does not, in itself, guarantee that we will experience a shift in consciousness. It will be experienced as a gift only if we choose to see and accept it as such. For myself, I could have chosen to remain in a disempowered, resentful state of mind when my old life dissolved. It was my search for greater meaning in what was happening that turned it into a blessing. It was not the situation itself. In fact, only after I allowed myself to feel the pain of loss was I able to move forward. I had come through a great challenge and chose to keep my heart open to the goodness of life. I chose to trust that everything that was happening to me was ultimately for my highest evolution. It was a process. If I had denied the painful feelings, I have no doubt that my life would have unfolded quite differently.

Disorientation

As your inner and outer structures begin to crumble, it is natural to experience some degree of disorientation. So, if you have been feeling disoriented, congratulations! It probably means that something in your world is crumbling and that you are reorienting yourself to a new way of being. As the old gives way to the new, you need to reorient yourself. You may have negative associations with the word disorientation. But, disorientation actually means that you are in the process of changing your orientation to yourself and the world. You let go of beliefs and mental frameworks that no longer serve you. You abandon old, ego-based identity. When you do this, you will probably feel some degree of disorientation. You may feel a sense of loss and the grief that goes with it. It is the same with the word disillusioned. Disillusionment means to let go of your illusions. This may feel uncomfortable, but it needs to happen in order to awaken to a new way of experiencing life.

This process of change and disintegration of the old might feel disturbing. It is, however, a positive indicator that the necessary inner transformation is occurring. Internal change needs to occur if we want to experience a new way of being in the world. If we truly want to experience *heaven on earth*, then major inner change and upheaval is unavoidable, and expected.

Heaven on Earth

Some people believe that heaven is a place we go to after our physical bodies die. Some say it's an experience of merging with or returning to source, once we have been released from our bodies. When I have asked people at Awakened Living gatherings what the word heaven means to them, they have said: bliss, oneness, no separation, connection, love, light, equality, trust, openheartedness, peace, freedom. If this is what heaven means to people, then I ask: Do we really have to wait until we die? What if we can choose that right now? What if we choose to cultivate these qualities, over their opposites? What would happen if each of us chose to be a living example of those qualities in our daily lives? What does it mean to live in heaven on earth? Is it possible that heaven on earth is something we inherently have the power to bring forth into our lives, right here and now, with no need to wait?

If we feel ready to leave the divided world behind, we can learn to embrace *all that is.* There is no other way. We don't need to separate and divide the world into "right and wrong," or "good and bad." We can reject that our mind is the highest source of knowing and listen to our intuition and our hearts. We can make the heart our new and permanent dwelling place. When we choose to live with an open heart, we can operate from an all-inclusive perspective.

Living openheartedly does not mean that we deny what we know to be true. It does not mean squelching our individuality. We have a clear, healthy sense of ourselves. It doesn't mean negating our unique, individual expression. It is actually quite the opposite. The more openhearted and loving we become, the more love we have for ourselves. The more love we have for ourselves, the more we honor and respect our own truth. We are authentic in our relationships with others. And the more authentic we are, the more we allow others to be *their* authentic selves.

When we live open-heartedly, as authentic expressions of the source of love we are, we can drop our fears and defenses. We know it is safe to reveal our true essence. Our internal conflict is over and there is no need for self-judgment, self-criticism, and self-attack. We experience the peace, freedom, love, and equality that *already exist* within us. *This is Heaven on Earth.* There is nothing we need to do, other than let go of the illusions we once believed to be true. *Heaven is already here.* We can simply open our eyes to its existence.

I invite you to make the choice, right now, to discover the heaven that already exists. I invite you to release everything in your life that does not support it. Let it fall away and accept this greater reality.

Spiritual Teachers

I want to say a few words about spiritual teachers. Most of us, at some point on our spiritual journey, benefit from the inspiration and support of a spiritual teacher. Having a teacher can be a valuable experience that accelerates our path of waking up to the truth of who we really are. A spiritual teacher can be an important reminder and a living model of our highest, awakened self. As such, teachers deserve our highest respect and gratitude for the role they play in our lives. However, when we put a spiritual teacher on a pedestal—and create a false, hierarchical division between us and our teacher—we keep ourselves locked in the world of separation. This is not helpful to the student or the teacher.

Waking up to the truth of who we truly are entails realizing our essential equality with all other human beings, including our teachers. At some point on our journey, we may want to acknowledge that we have the potential to embody all the qualities that our teacher has demonstrated. There is no hierarchy, no higher and lower. However, in order to realize our true nature, we will want to release all our existing, false identities. We simply let go of our limited notions about who and what we are, and fully realize the truth of our being. Our true identity is revealed once we are willing to dismantle all known ideas of who we are.

A small word of caution: We do not want to expand our ego into a grandiose version of itself. Nothing is less appealing than spiritual arrogance or spiritual righteousness. I know too well what can happen when ego starts to believe itself to be spirit. Adyashanti, the American spiritual teacher and writer, says it perfectly: "*There are few things more distorted or dangerous than an ego that thinks it is God.*"

Freedom from Addiction

For those dealing with addiction, when they surrender the addiction, something powerful happens. They let go of a major block. The kingdom of heaven already exists. So, when someone releases their addiction, when they surrender, they realize the truth of who they are. Nothing is more painful than 99 percent surrender. And for a lot of people in an addiction, they live in that 99 percent surrender—often for years. Finally, when that moment happens, and they walk into a treatment center or a counselor's office, and are ready to stop the addictive behavior, something powerful occurs simply by having the willingness to let go. And what's left? Heaven.

Personal Accountability

An important aspect of creating heaven on earth is that we understand *we are absolutely accountable for our own reality*. We are accountable for our responses to life, for our behavior. We are accountable for how we show up in the world—the words we speak, our attitudes and beliefs. Though many of our behaviors and beliefs were absorbed unconsciously from the world around us, as we awaken, we become more and more conscious. We become conscious of our habits, our conditioning, and what is still unresolved or unhealed within us from the past. Our unconsciousness can cause us to behave in ways that, on a conscious level, we would not do. We become reactive when we don't want to.

It may feel like a burden and an enormous amount of work to transform our unwanted patterns of behavior. However, as long as we unconsciously re-create the same old problems and issues from our past, we will continue to suffer. We will believe that something outside us is controlling our life. As we do the work of growing our level of consciousness, it's important we have an attitude of patience and compassion for ourselves. It does not serve us to make ourselves "wrong" for who we have been or who we are today. Having compassion for the path we have taken, means there is no need for self-condemnation. We understand that everything in our life is unfolding exactly as it needs to.

Dr. Wayne Dyer, an author and speaker in the fields of self-development and spiritual growth, said, *"Heaven on Earth is a choice you must make, not a place you must find."*

Each of us has the power to create a state of heaven on earth, right here, right now. Are you ready?

Chapter Six

AWAKE WITHIN THE DREAM

"Everything, seen in itself, is both good and bad, right and wrong, useful and useless, appropriate and inappropriate, possible and beyond possibility. A battering ram can break down a city wall, but it cannot patch a hole in the ceiling. Fine horses can travel a hundred miles in a day, but they can't catch mice as a weasel can. The owl can spot a flea in the dark, but in broad daylight, however hard it may stare, it can't even see a mountain. If you want to have right without wrong or order without disorder, you don't understand the Tao. You can't have one quality and not have its opposite as well. You can't reach for the positive and not create the negative by the very act of your reaching. The Master stands beyond opposites. She doesn't move toward or away. She sees things exactly as they are."

— *Excerpt from* The Second Book of the Tao, *by Stephen Mitchell*

The Persistence of Illusion

What is reality? Is it possible we are all dreaming? Is it possible that "reality" is not as solid as we once believed? If so, what if we could change the dream? Perhaps the intention in recognizing the illusory nature of life is not to attempt to wake up from the dream, but to wake up *within* the dream. Eckhart Tolle says it this way in his book, *A New Earth*: "*When we are awake within the dream, the ego-created earth-drama comes to an end and a more benign and wondrous dream arises.*" Waking up to our essential nature does not forgo the reality that we still live in the world as a seemingly separate individual. The difference is that, when awakened, we are no longer *only* indentified with being a separate self. We also see ourselves as one with all creation. When we are spiritually awakened, the personality serves as an instrument of spirit, rather than the ego running the show.

Glimpses into Ultimate Reality

Most of us, at some point, have had unexpected glimpses and awareness of our true essence. That glimpse might have lasted for a few seconds, a few hours, or for days or weeks. In that moment of awakening, the illusion of separation fell away. More often than not, however, the ego mind probably stepped back in to reclaim its control. However, if we were to remain the observer of the ego's voice, we would have been less easily drawn back into re-identifying with it.

I have had several such experiences in my own life, most notably when I traveled to India in 2006. I had been in the darkest period of my life, which started over a year earlier, when I had participated in all sorts of harm of myself and others and ultimately lost everything I owned. I had been doing the deep work of "soul searching" during that time. I was with a group on a spiritual journey that ended in Varanasi. If you are not familiar with Varanasi, it is a city in the northern part of India on the bank of the Ganges River. Many Hindus believe if you die there, your karma will be removed and you will not need to be reincarnated.

So, needless to say, the experience of death is all around. Varanasi is more than 10, 000 years old and is the oldest city in the world that has been continuously inhabited by humans.

In the oldest parts of the city, roads are too narrow for cars, so we approached the city by bicycle rickshaw. I could feel the spiritual energy intensifying as we approached. A chill went up my arms, and my heart began to open in a way I had rarely experienced. Once we reached the oldest part of the city, we were escorted on foot by twin deaf boys who seemed to be about 12 years old. Their gentle energies were incredibly striking. We reached the river bank, where the Ganga Aarti, known as the festival of lights, was under way. This festival happens every evening in Varanasi at sundown. There were seven tall platforms along the river bank, each with a priest facing the river paying tribute to the mighty Ganges.

We boarded a boat and floated out onto the river. A profound peace entered my body and, in that moment, my ego was stripped away. I sobbed uncontrollably for nearly an hour. Suddenly, the electrical power went out and shrouded half of the city in darkness (not uncommon in many parts of India). The only things that lit up the night sky were the bodies burning in the ghats along the river. Our guides quietly steered the boat over to the ghat and we sat there, for what seemed like an eternity, watching the funeral ceremonies. We were only a few feet away from a burning body. The flames filled up the otherwise dark night with beautiful, sparkling light. The experience of my sudden awakening lasted with that intensity for several hours.

I awoke the next morning to discover my life had permanently shifted into a new way of being. Since that experience, my ego has continued to make its appearance in my life, but that moment allowed me to have a permanent change in my *relationship* with ego. My ego did not die, I simply changed the way I see it and the way it plays a role in my life. As Dr. Sue Morter, international speaker, master of bio-energetic medicine, and quantum field visionary, so eloquently states: "*Only ego would want ego to die.*"

The Power of Perspective

Stillness is found beyond the thinking mind, and beyond all the dualities that the mind creates. When we enter stillness we step outside of the world of "good and bad," or "right and wrong." In the stillness there are no judgments or opinions. Neither is there any particular meaning to what happens in our outer lives. There's just *what is.* When we become still, we tap into the eternal, changeless dimension within ourselves. And from that place there is a clear witnessing of the events of our lives. We experience a freedom to create our own interpretation, to make our own meaning—or not—around what we perceive is happening in our personal world, and the world at large.

In this sense, we all live in our personally constructed reality. Two people observing the same event, or having the same experience, might draw very different conclusions. They will find different meaning in that same experience. And the same person will most likely find different meaning in the same experience at different times in their life. The aspect of mind that's always becoming, changing, and learning—the part that exists *in time*— sees things from a different perspective at age 50 than it did when it was 25 or 5 years old.

If a loved one or somebody in my family has a serious illness, or dies, how I relate to that is all a matter of my perspective. When I access that part of me that exists *outside of time*—the ultimate observer—I see there's actually no meaning to it apart from the story that I tell in my mind. There's no inherent meaning to illness or death. And so, I'm free to create my inner experience, my inner reality, moment to moment as I choose the meaning I give to the events that unfold in my life. And beyond all the stories my mind creates, there's just *what is*. I am not the sum total of my circumstances, but the meaning I give to those experiences.

Blessing or Curse?

Whatever story we tell ourselves, and believe, is what we experience as the truth of what is happening. The more conscious awareness we have, the more we realize that the stories are self-created. For example, we are at liberty to decide whether an illness is a gift or a curse. We *decide* if losing a loved one is a tragic experience or an opportunity for miraculous transformation. Either way, we will still feel grief and loss, but suffering, which is very different from pain, is a choice. Losing our job can be a demeaning, humiliating experience or an invitation to live the life we always dreamed of but were afraid to step into. It is for each of us to decide whether the world we live in is a kind, loving place or a hostile, scary one. Whichever story we believe, our mind will find all the evidence it needs to prove us right.

Some people say, "Everything happens for a reason." If they arrived late at the airport and missed their flight, they rationalize it by telling themselves there was a reason. They say there was a higher purpose to why that happened. When they believe this, it makes it easier for them to accept the less fortunate things that occur. It's comforting to know that something good will come from misfortune. It is certainly more comfortable than believing that things happen randomly and that there is no intelligent organizing principle controlling the events of their lives. What I am saying is that perhaps neither of these two attitudes is actually true. At the very least, it may not be the whole truth. Events are not handed to us in a gift box nicely wrapped up with a bow. Rather it is *up to us* to create our own meaning.

Additionally, life can even be experienced *beyond* the trappings of meaning-making. For example, it is freeing to have no attachments to whether it is a sunny or a rainy day, whether we are tall or short. This is the Buddhist concept of nonattachment. When this dimension within us has been awakened, there is a deep sense of freedom. It cannot be experienced from a place of holding on to all our stories and opinions. I have lived through some dark experiences. During those times, I wanted to tell myself that it was all happening "for a reason." I did a lot of inner reflection around those difficult experiences and chose to use them as material for my transformation. And I created reason and meaning for those times of struggle. However, this was because of my deep commitment to personal growth and spiritual awakening. I could have chosen to be resentful, remorseful or angry and remain in a state of disempowerment. Inherently, these experiences were neither good nor bad. It was entirely my choice to view them in a positive light, to find constructive meaning and purpose in them.

Evidence or Conclusion?

Most of us are taught that we come to a conclusion by gathering evidence. If we look at the "facts" of a situation, we will be able to determine the correct conclusion. Our entire legal system is based on this, and many in the scientific community adhere to this structure of knowing as well. I invite you to turn that concept on its head and begin to question this assumption. Is it possible that the reverse of this formula is actually true? Perhaps you come to a conclusion and then go about finding evidence to support that conclusion. This is often the case in our legal system, and quantum physics is now revealing this reality in the scientific field as well. The observer has an effect. In our personal lives, we may encounter situations which repeat themselves over and over. We can look to evidence to support our position. Or, we can pause and examine our conclusions and see what happens when we focus on changing that instead. In my experience, miraculous changes occur simply by looking at my assumptions and making the inner shift to a different way of seeing the world.

If we decide that some things in life are "good," and some are "bad," then we find ourselves living in a dualistic world where we need to be careful and keep ourselves safe. In this reality, things can go wrong, people can be hurtful, and we need to protect ourselves from those who want to harm us and from the evils of life. We can find plenty of evidence to confirm this reality. I'm not saying that we should ignore the world around us. We can, however, be aware of and act in accordance with our inner truth. In the end, it is up to each of us to decide what kind of world we live in. We don't need to wait for anything to change on the outside before we can inhabit the world of our choice. What kind of world are you choosing to see today?

We can choose to recognize that everything that happens to us is useful for our awakening, and that it contributes to our well-being and our wholeness. We step into in a world where nothing is actually against us. In this reality, there are no enemies. It is safe to befriend the here and now, and we can trust that whatever is happening in this moment can serve our highest spiritual development. Whatever happened in our past also served our highest spiritual development. In this way, we can have a daily living experience of being *at one with* the rest of life. We can know ourselves as part of the seamless fabric of existence. In fact, this is the only way we can experience our oneness with all that is, and tap into the profound sense of peace and harmony that already exists deep within us. Letting go of our stories is the shortcut to living in a peaceful world.

Death and Rebirth

In the 1980s and early 1990s, when many people in this country were dying from AIDS, I witnessed time and again how people's diagnosis took them in one of two directions. Some became angry, shut down, and closed off. Others allowed the experience to open them up in the most miraculous way. Their inner radiance shone through them and lifted them up into an expanded state of consciousness. The way they chose to view their diagnosis informed how they experienced it. Some decided that, whatever time they had remaining, they were going to make the most of it and connect through love, while others felt like they were victims to a needless disease. It is easy to see how both perspectives are valid, but also clear to see what happens in our lives based on how we view the world.

Another powerful example of this happened some years back, when I ran into an old friend who had clearly gone through a dramatic transformation. Previous to that moment, I had experienced him as one of the most bitter, resentful people I had ever known. He lived in an unsafe world where other people were out to get him. When I bumped into him, I was amazed to see how he had changed. His entire aura was transformed. When I asked him what had happened, he pointed down and I realized that he was now missing a leg. This experience of losing his leg had been a huge catalyst of transformation for him. It was not losing his leg that caused the shift in him. It was *what he decided to do* with that experience. From his loss, he had turned bitterness and fear into joy and love.

Leaning In

I must admit that I spent much of my earlier life trying to avoid the uncomfortable parts of my life. Many of us do the same. I was running away from "the human experience." In those days, I tried every possible distraction I could think of to avoid my feelings. I turned to addictions of all kinds—anything to avoid the present moment and my disturbing emotions. I had no idea how to handle my feelings. As a child, I never learned how to cope with difficult and intense emotions. And I was never taught—either at home or at school—that beneath those difficult feelings, I was essentially OK; that I was actually a perfect expression of life. Over time, I had to learn that difficult emotions were a perfectly natural expression of the human and spiritual experience.

In her book, *When Things Fall Apart*, Pema Chodron speaks about this human tendency to run away from uncomfortable feelings. She advises us to move toward them, to open up to them, rather than running away: *"Through meditation we're able to see clearly what's going on with our thoughts and emotions and we can also let them go. What's encouraging about meditation is that even when we shut down, we can no longer shut down in ignorance. We see very clearly that we're closing off. That in itself begins to illuminate the darkness of ignorance. We're able to see how we run and hide and keep ourselves busy so that we never have to let our hearts be penetrated. And we're also able to see how we can open and relax. Basically disappointment, embarrassment, in all these places where we just cannot feel good, are a sort of death."*

In moments of discomfort I can remember that I have a choice in how I perceive what is happening. If I am able to access the stillness within, I can watch the movement of events without judgment or ideas about "rightness" or "wrongness." From this place I am *one with* the movement, in fact *I am* the movement itself. And as I allow myself to be the movement—while being the observer and the one who experiences it—I come to understand these different aspects of my being. I move in and out of these aspects many times during the day; in and out of the personal and the transcendent.

Fear of Dying

I once read an interview with Dr. Maya Angelou. In the article, she said that the moment she totally came to terms with the fact that she was going to die she had an immediate shift of consciousness. She recognized that life was precious, and she began to dedicate herself to giving and living more fully. Perhaps if more of us could come to this kind of understanding, there would be less fear in our culture around dying, and more gratitude for purposeful living.

I think it is interesting how American society is obsessed with trying to avoid death. This culture is addicted to the idea of staying young. We spend hundreds of thousands of dollars on beauty products, face-lifts, and painful plastic surgeries in an attempt to remain looking perfect forever. Not that I haven't bought into some of this kind of thinking myself, but I believe it is important to acknowledge that underlying this obsession may be our fear of death. Many of us fear the death of our physical body. And many also fear the loss of something we have become identified with. It might be our looks, our youthfulness, our material possessions, our partner, our job, or even our spiritual community and the spiritual practices in which we engage. We may even fear losing our perspectives or mental structures of knowing. Many of us are strongly identified with our belief systems. But even the content of our mind is form. It's thought-form. And it changes over time. It is not the truth of who we really are—the unchangeable, eternal self—that we can only come to know in the stillness.

I had an intense period of death and rebirth a few years before I became a spiritual teacher. When I first became aware that ministry was my path, I felt a deep resistance. I did not want to acknowledge it. I did everything I could to push this inner knowing back down. I tried desperately to steer my life in a different direction. I started one business after another in an attempt to avoid what I knew I needed to do. Each new business collapsed within a short period of time. I resisted and judged what was happening to me, making myself "wrong" for not succeeding. And, because I was unwilling to let go of my deeply entrenched ego, I harmed others by my recklessness and unconscious behavior. It was an extremely painful period of my life. Only when I let go of how I thought my life "should" look was I able to accept the new life that wanted to be born through me. I had to allow my self-concepts to die. Only after that was I able to allow the new beginning, which had made itself known to me.

There is no avoiding the fact that a death of some sort needs to happen before lasting transformation can take place. Old ways of being need to be released in order to make way for the new. Throughout our lives, we pass through these natural cycles of ego-death and rebirth. As we let go of the old, we are reborn into a new way of being in the world. We have a new way of experiencing ourselves and a new way of seeing the world. We can move through these cycles either willingly or we can meet them with resistance. The choice is ours. And of course, the more we resist these organic movements of our lives, the more we suffer.

Serving Others

As the minister of Awakened Living, I am sometimes asked about my views regarding doing "good" in the world. Someone recently said that if I truly cared about the tragedies occurring in the world, then I would do something practical to help the oppressed and needy people. This person suggested I had been spending my time navel-gazing. My response is that, as individuals, we are each called to make a difference in the world in our own unique way. Every one of us has particular gifts and strengths that we can choose to use to help relieve the suffering of others. We each have our unique purpose to fulfill. There is no "one size fits all" answer when it comes to contributing to the greater good of humanity.

A model I find useful is to recognize the four levels of how we operate in the world, as discussed in chapter four of this book. At level one, we may feel overwhelmed with the seeming injustice in the world and experience a deep sense of anger, sadness, or powerlessness. We see the people we are trying to help as victims and we are filled with the need to make it "right." At level two we are primarily concerned with taking care of our own needs. Maybe we desire fame, fortune, and success to boost our sense of self. The needs of others are not at the forefront of our awareness. We rarely participate in social action, other than perhaps making financial contributions to worthy causes. At the third level, our focus shifts again to helping others, and we are compelled to do "good" in the world. However we don't see those we serve as victims, we see them as fellow humans in need of support. Our intention is to be of service and offer a helping hand. We might offer assistance as a mentor or create educational courses that allow people to help themselves.

This is a noble way to serve, yet there is another level—the fourth level—which is not about what we are *doing*, but about who we are *being*. It is about what we are contributing at the level of consciousness. In no way am I saying that once we reach this level, we no longer serve in the ways previously mentioned. It just means that our *primary* way of serving is by assisting people to raise awareness and consciousness, predominantly by tending to our own spiritual being-ness. At this level, the highest contribution you can make is to allow the world to be *as it is*, and have compassion for the state it is in. There is no desire to "fix" it, because you know no one is *broken*. You deeply understand your oneness with it and allow yourself to be moved into action—or not—from this place of connectedness. You trust that your inner knowing will guide you to your rightful place in the world, whatever that might be. Perhaps you will be guided to work in very practical ways to create positive changes for mankind, at the level of consciousness.

Your inner knowing might tell you to join the Peace Corps, or create a nonprofit to help the homeless. Or maybe it will guide you to stay in your job and support your family. Perhaps it will instruct you to travel to India and spend time in an ashram, or pack up your things and travel around the world. Only you can truly know what is yours to do. Spending time in the stillness helps to clarify what your outer calling is. You can trust your inner knowing enough to act on it. Are you still living in a world of "good and bad" while believing that you know how others "should" be living their lives?

When we truly know who we are—and our actions come from that place of connectedness with all that is—we cannot help but act from love. From here, it's automatic that what we do is useful for the whole because we are *being love*. There's no need to "do good" because the terms "good" and "bad" have lost their meaning. Everything we do emanates love into the world and enhances the feeling of connectedness. If everybody knew themselves at this level, there would *be* no starvation, no cruelty, no wars, no poverty, and no inequality. It is our divided state of consciousness that creates these issues in the first place. Imagine a world where all human beings knew themselves to be pure love—and acted accordingly—what would happen to the world's problems? We are often asked to monitor our carbon footprint. I am asking each of us to also reflect on and adjust our "spiritual footprint." How we behave has a ripple effect that can and will change the world.

Rumi beautifully stated it in this way: *"Out beyond ideas of wrongdoing and rightdoing there is a field. I'll meet you there."*

Chapter Seven

LIVING ON PURPOSE

"Your life has an inner purpose and an outer purpose. Inner purpose concerns Being and is primary. Outer purpose concerns doing and it is secondary. Your inner purpose is to awaken. It is as simple as that....Finding and living in alignment with your inner purpose is the foundation for fulfilling your outer purpose. It's the basis for true success."

— *Excerpt from* A New Earth, *by Eckhart Tolle*

Doing and Being

In our action-oriented society, people tend to think of their purpose as solely an external activity. When asked "What is your purpose in life?" most people say it is about the roles they play, or want to play, in the world. Some say they want to be a good mother, or a loving and supportive husband. Others say they hope to be successful in their career, or to fulfill certain goals and dreams. Rarely does it occur to them to take a step back and connect with their state of *being* first, before concerning themselves with *doing*.

The experiences of my earlier life taught me that if my *doing* is not fully grounded in my *being*, then it is like building a house on sand rather than on solid ground. Another way of saying this is that *conscious being* naturally gives rise to *conscious doing*. I used to believe that if I could figure out what was mine to *do* in life, and if I successfully accomplished it, then I would *be* living on purpose. Consequently I would feel fulfilled. So I spent my early years building what I thought was "the life of my dreams." That included a successful career along with the external trappings I thought I needed. I believed I was living my purpose. However it was not long before everything I had worked so hard toward came tumbling down. In retrospect, I realize that during that period, my *doing* was primarily divorced from my *being*. The life I had strived so hard to build fell apart because there was no solid foundation beneath it.

Inner and Outer Purpose

Once I had done the deep inner work of discovering *who I truly am*—and developed the ability to reside in that in my daily life—then my *doing* emerged easily and organically from that internal place of stability. When I am connected to *who I am*, as spirit, there is no longer any sense of personal struggle or effort. Struggle and effort are only needed when I lose touch with my authentic being. When I'm rooted in being, communication channels from within are intact and I am informed and guided by a deep sense of knowing. The actions I need to take become clear and obvious, moment to moment.

In American culture, it seems perfectly normal to be more concerned with *doing* than with *being*. Our society is dominated by left-brained logic. Subtle, intuitive messages come to us through different channels and are often drowned out by the loud noise of our logical minds. Given that we have lived in a logic-dominated world for several thousand years, many of us do not question this way of functioning. However, when we acknowledge the multiple crises that are currently affecting life on our planet, it becomes clear that we are blindly letting our limited, logical minds rule our lives. This is no longer sustainable. We need to find another way. Regular meditation or quiet time carves out some inner space. It provides the inner silence in which the still, small voice within can be heard. The more we pay attention, and are willing to listen to this gentle voice of guidance, the stronger and more reliable it becomes.

In my daily life, I remember that my primary purpose is to remain connected to being. I live in a state of openhearted, vulnerable, authenticity. This means I'm willing to listen to the communications that come from all aspects of my being—mind, body, heart, and spirit. I am committed to having my mind "step down" from its elevated, autocratic position. As I allow myself to be guided from within, I find that my external life flows with an effortless ease. This is not to say I don't have moments of stress, difficulty, or confusion. But when I do, I realize that it is because my mind has taken control again. And all I need to do is remember to relinquish my mind's control and to return to *being*, as my primary purpose. With that remembrance, tension instantly dissolves and I am able to return to my naturally joyous state.

Head and Heart

It has been said that the journey from the head to the heart is the longest 18-inch journey we will ever take. This journey, however, is possibly the most important passage of our lives. Albert Einstein understood that we could tap into our highest source of intelligence. He said, *"The intuitive mind is a sacred gift and the rational mind is a faithful servant. We have created a society that honors the servant and has forgotten the gift."* Einstein was way ahead of his time. He indicated that we need to shift our sense of loyalty to the intuitive mind, to the heart. Rather than making our rational mind our supreme source of understanding, we can honor the heart's understanding. At this level, we can tap into a far greater knowing—the knowing of the whole—rather than merely the knowing of our separated mind.

Considering the current state of humanity, perhaps we are ready to acknowledge that we have gone as far as we can without honoring the sacred gift of our intuition, our higher knowing. We realize that it is time to train and discipline our logical minds so that they can play their intended role. The mind is a powerful tool and when utilized as a faithful servant, great accomplishments are achieved. It is when we believe that we *are* our minds (or our thoughts) that difficulty and discord arise.

Conflict between the mind and the heart primarily arises when the mind wants to dominate. Why is the intelligence of the heart a higher intelligence than that of the mind? Because heart intelligence comes from a place of connectedness. It is at the level of the heart that we have the capacity to feel and know our oneness with the whole of life. Our mind's intelligence comes from the perspective of our separateness. It is vital that we honor and respect our individuality. However if we want to survive as a species, and to experience our inherent interconnectivity, then we need to leave behind our old structures of knowing where we believed the mind was our highest source of intelligence. We need to transcend to a new structure of knowing. This means living from the heart and trusting it as a higher source of intelligence. The heart I am referring to is not only the emotional heart, but the absolute connection with our intuitive nature. The survival of our planet is at stake here. And we now possess the potential for all of us to raise our consciousness and live lives filled with peace and love.

Knowing Our Outer Purpose

Spirit manifests uniquely in each of us. We all find and walk our own path through life. But how do we find clarity about our individual purpose? Recently, during a workshop I was facilitating, I asked a participant, "What do you absolutely know you are here to do?" At the time, she was feeling extremely frustrated in the workplace. Although she was enjoying a high corporate salary, she hated every minute of her job. She said. "The only thing I know I'm here to do is to help animals." It was clear to me that she had gotten in touch with her life's calling, based on how she lit up when speaking this and by the conviction in her voice. However she immediately discounted the idea, saying, "But I can't do that. I'm not going to veterinary school, and I'm not even sure that's what I mean by helping animals. And there's no way I could possibly make a living doing that anyway." Her purpose had emerged, for a split second, and then her mind totally dismissed it. It was a clear example of how we allow our logical minds to dominate us. We have learned to allow the limited thinking patterns of our brain to control our behavior. And in the process, we have lost an enormous amount of our potential for joy. I believe that our heart knows what our purpose is. And when we are willing to quiet our mind and listen to our heart's wisdom, it can guide us in a useful direction. And we can trust that direction to be correct if it increases our joy.

It was during a workshop led by Diane Conway, author of the book *What Would You Do If You Had No Fear?* that I first gave voice to my calling to be a spiritual teacher. At the workshop, Diane asked me the powerful question which is also the title of her book. And for the first time, I acknowledged and spoke out loud my desire to work in the arena of ministry and spiritual counseling. It was a big "aha" moment for me. I felt as though a spark was ignited the moment I shared this deep knowing with the other participants in the room.

At the time I owned a furniture store and designed my own line of furniture. I wasn't sure how I would make the transition from store owner to doing spiritual work. People at the workshop were eager to support me with their ideas and offered suggestions about how I could combine the two careers. Someone recommended that I make "spiritual furniture" by infusing positive energy into the pieces. It was difficult for them to imagine that I would give up my successful furniture business and step into a completely new field of work. It was an example of how logic can take hold of an inspired idea and immediately limit the possibility of fulfilling it. The logical mind can only think within the limits of what is already known. Listening to other people's ideas about how I might fulfill my calling was a somewhat frustrating experience. It kept me trapped within the confines of logical thought and of the past. I was relieved when Diane looked at me and said, "I hear you, TJ...and I know it's not about furniture. Give yourself full permission to continue freely exploring this idea." What a priceless gift she offered me that day.

Nurturing Our Purpose

Once we have discovered what our purpose is, it is important to keep it safe from instant dismissal from our logical mind. Like a newly planted sapling, our new purpose needs gentle nurturing for it to safely grow and take root. It might be wise to share our goals only with those people who understand the delicate process of delivering and growing a new idea. In my case, the next step was to have a conversation with someone who was already a spiritual counselor. That person gave me helpful support and guidance. But then my mind started to intimidate me, asking questions like: "Who are *you* to do that kind of work?" Our minds can act as bullies to the more subtle, gentle voices of our heart and intuition. If someone else intimidated us that way, it would be a clear act of abuse. But do we recognize abuse when it comes from within our mind and is directed against the subtler voices of our heart or intuition? I have heard it stated: "My mind is a dangerous neighborhood that I should try to avoid."

In praise of the logical mind, it does an excellent job of processing information, sorting, organizing, and categorizing. It is an essential tool when it comes to implementing action steps. But if we rely on our logic too early in the creative process, it will prevent us from discovering the steps that will lead us into new territory. Again, we can find wisdom in Einstein's words: "*Imagination is more important than knowledge, for knowledge is limited to all we now know and understand, while imagination embraces the entire world, and all there ever will be to know and understand.*"

To manifest our outer purpose, it is important to remind ourselves of what our purpose is. We need to begin living in the "vibration" of it, even before it has manifested. It is all too easy to get lost in attempting to figure out "How do I do it?" Instead we will want to move into the already-existing energy of it, which can be found within us. By embodying the vibration of our purpose, we become magnetic to the people, opportunities, and situations that will enable us to make our purpose manifest. When I stepped into the feeling tone of assisting people with their spiritual transformation, I knew I was energetically opening doors for this new work to be born. I then took consistent and determined action in the desirable direction and inevitably the physical world responded. Suddenly opportunities appeared that matched the vibration in which I was already living. It was a truly magical process and I am deeply grateful to be living my purpose.

Purposeful Living

Some people are born with a strong calling and are aware from a young age what they are here to do. But the Mozarts of this world are in the minority. Most of us have multiple steps or layers to our calling. One step leads to the next, in a gradual unfolding. The connection between these steps might not be obvious until we look back and connect the dots and trace our progression. There is no one-size-fits-all formula for finding and living our purpose. Many of us feel inner resistance, in the form of fear, as we get in touch with our deepest calling. However, we can cultivate the courage to work with and overcome these inner roadblocks and move forward. It is a process and a journey, which we each engage in our unique way. We ask for support when we need it. My own experience has shown me that we often have to do deep and difficult internal work to overcome our fears. It is that process of transformation that enables us to fulfill our calling. Our personal development deepens as we continue to live on purpose and take each next step that we find before us.

Living on purpose, or living an intentional life, is achieved when we find the right balance between *being* and *doing*. It is the yin and yang of our existence. Our being feeds and energizes our doing. Conversely, if we put too much emphasis on being, and not enough on doing, then nothing gets accomplished in the outer realm. We lack engagement with the world, and we may experience dissatisfaction. When we obsessively *do*, without paying attention to being, what we do loses its sense of meaningfulness and connectedness to the larger web of life.

Right Brain Magnificence

Dr. Jill Bolte Taylor, a brain scientist who had a stroke that caused her left brain to completely shut down, has explained what the right brain is capable of perceiving when its vision is not obscured by our logical mind. As a brain researcher, she was cognizant of what was occurring to her, while it was happening. Her stroke caused her left brain to go totally silent. In her own words: *"I was immediately captivated by the magnificence of energy around me. And because I could no longer identify the boundaries of my body, I felt enormous and expansive. I felt at one with all the energy that was, and it was beautiful."*

She described the state as nirvana, and she knew, in that moment, that everyone was capable of experiencing it. She glimpsed the possibility of a world full of compassionate, loving people; those who could move into that expansive sense of well-being, perfection, and oneness. It was possible at any time they chose by purposely stepping into the right hemisphere of their brain. (What we often refer to as the heart) She added, *"My left brain is doing the best job it can with the information it has to work with. I need to remember, however, that there are enormous gaps between what I know and what I think I know."*

Jill further states that *"The more time we spend choosing to run the deep inner peace circuitry of our right hemispheres, the more peace we will project into the world and the more peaceful our planet will be."* Sharing this message with others is what motivated Jill to spend the next eight years of her life working to heal and recover her ability to walk, talk, read and write, and recall the details of her earlier life. She made a full recovery and tells her incredible story in her book *My Stroke of Insight*. Fortunately, most of us do not need to have a stroke to glimpse the magnificence of right brain perception. When we quiet our dominant logical minds, the voices of our heart and intuition can be heard. It will open doors to see what life is like from an integrated, whole-brain perspective.

Chapter Eight

FINDING TRUE LOVE

"The course does not aim at teaching the meaning of love, for that is beyond what can be taught. It does aim, however, at removing the blocks to the awareness of love's presence, which is your natural inheritance. The opposite of love is fear, but what is all-encompassing can have no opposite."
— *Excerpt from* A Course in Miracles

Love Is What We Are

If you look into the eyes of a newborn baby, you will recognize its profound wholeness. One cannot deny the pristine perfection of new life. We seem to come into this world inherently perfect and whole. We are born, as love. However, as we grow up, we learn the ways of the world. We are taught belief systems that are contradictory to our original knowing. In our formative years, we adopt psychological survival mechanisms to deal with the difficulties we encounter. When we suffer from emotional wounds, we close down in order to protect ourselves from further hurt. I have come to recognize and reframe these coping mechanisms as brilliant strategies for survival. The issue for us is that these strategies have become maladaptive. What was once a brilliant strategy is now keeping us imprisoned in a way of being that is no longer serving us. Marianne Williamson says it this way: *"Love is what we're born with, fear is what we are taught."* In learning about fear—the need for which arises from a belief system that tells us we are separate from each other and the world—we forget our true essence.

I remember the moment I forgot the truth of who I was. I was seven years old. I remember the physical sensation of shutting down. I was overcome with feeling the need to close off my heart. It no longer felt safe to keep it open. I started believing the stories the adults in my life were unconsciously teaching me: Some people are better than others, some are worse; some are good, and some are bad. I started believing in the idea of separation, the concept of right and wrong. And I also became aware of suffering and violence. I felt overwhelmed and decided the world was not safe and that I needed to protect myself. I also decided that something was wrong with *me* and I was not enough. At that early age I had begun to feel and experience myself and the world as spiritually bankrupt. Because of that, I started to look outside myself to fill the inner emptiness. Over the years, as I grew into a young adult, I did what most of us do—I tried to plug myself into many different things—including romantic partners, money, clothes, prestige etc. It was an attempt to reconnect to myself and feel loved. As a young boy, and as a young adult, I didn't realize that it was my closed-off heart that was causing me to feel an inner sense of lack.

The Search for Romantic Love

Many of us believe the fairy tale that somebody will arrive and give us a love that will make us feel whole and complete. As in a movie, we believe in the fantasy that someone will magically appear and fill our emptiness. It is absolutely natural for us to desire a romantic partner. However when we expect that partner to fill our emptiness, our inner void, then we create a relationship based on dependency, and on fear of loss. We create a relationship with an unstable foundation, because it's based on a fundamental lie about who we are. Only when we have remembered ourselves to *be* love, do we have a dependable, lasting source *of* love to share with another. The reality is that nobody *needs* a partner in order to be happy. It's the disconnection from our true essence that creates the misperception that somebody else needs to supply us with love.

As an exercise in one of my workshops, I ask participants to write down what it is they are looking for in a partner. Next, I have them write three things—usually feelings—they think that partner will bring them. Then, I ask them, "Do you think it's possible that you already possess those feelings and qualities? Do you see that you already *are* that?" If we delve inside of ourselves, we can find all the qualities we think a relationship will give us. Ultimately, the real reason we want a relationship is so we can *express* our wholeness, and have people reflect it back to us. When we truly know ourselves to *be* love, we create relationships where we mirror back our true essence to each other. If we desire a healthy and sustainable relationship, we will want to be with a partner who also knows that truth about herself or himself.

In working with people who are looking for a partner, I am often asked, "Why do I keep attracting unavailable people?" A more useful question might be, "Why are you attracted *to* unavailable people?" Ironically, there is actually a gift in recognizing you are attracted to unavailable people. They reflect to you where you are not fully available to *yourself*, and where you are not fully available to love another. I then usually ask: "What do you want them to be available *for*?" If you are seeking another person to do your inner work for you, then the relationship is not sustainable. A couple questions that might be useful: How can you be more fully available to yourself? How can you be more fully available to the love that is already present, inside of you? When you truly know yourself to *be* love, there will never be any shortage of love. You will know yourself to be forever one with an infinite supply of love that is unconditional. Then a relationship becomes about sharing love rather than seeking love from another. Isn't this what we all most want?

The Great Remembering

The journey to consciously knowing your original perfection and wholeness begins with a decision. It begins with a desire and a willingness to know, beyond a shadow of a doubt, that *love is who you are*. There is a world of difference between looking for love on the outside, and discovering your inner essence, which *is* love. Once it is discovered, you can live your life as an authentic example of that love. Your mind might think it's a nice idea to know yourself as love. However it takes a sincere commitment to overcome the inner resistances you inevitably encounter on this journey. You need to clear out everything that is counter to that. It takes enormous courage and stamina to dismantle the inner obstacles that have prevented you from seeing yourself as love.

This journey involves unearthing yourself from the multiple layers of illusion and confusion that cover your core essence. It necessitates that you dis-identify with everything in you that *isn't* loving. But first you have to understand and have compassion for it. In my experience, I remained stuck in painful patterns until it became more painful than changing. Only then did I become willing to try a new approach. Life is like that.

On your journey of self-remembering, you ought to dismantle the beliefs that obscure knowing yourself to be pure love. I like to call it The Great Remembering. Along the way, you may find all the self-doubt, self-criticism, self-judgment, and anything else that would tell you otherwise. You are excavating the brilliant shining light that you truly are, at your core. This light becomes more and more exposed as you remove what has covered it.

There are many tools and techniques that can help you dismantle the false information you have accumulated about yourself. What matters most is that you choose something that is effective for you, and use it. You might want to meet with a spiritual coach or counselor, spend time in meditation, or join a supportive spiritual community. These and other things may assist you in the process. You will know it's working when you begin to feel your old, limited sense of self diminishing, and your more expansive, authentic self beginning to freely emerge.

Meditation can be an invaluable tool for you on your journey of self-discovery. It enables you to cut through the more superficial layers of the thinking mind and drop down deeper within. Only by moving beyond thought can you begin to experience the more expansive, unchanging essence of who you truly are. Take some quiet time and sit in the silence. Focus on your essential nature or energy field that is beyond the constructs of your mind. You will start to reach deeper into your essential knowing, and make contact with your original self.

Support for Your Undoing

Although not essential, you might want to work with a counselor, therapist, or spiritual coach. They can help clear your mind of old structures that you are ready to be let go of. Your ego-mind may have some resistance to this process. The ego's role is to preserve the status quo. It resists change. If you decide to work with a professional, trust your intuitive sense about who you choose. In doing psycho-spiritual work, it is important to select someone who feels like a good match. It's important to have a safe place to explore and dismantle the inner workings of your mental and emotional make-up. You may discover that you have been identifying with something other than love. When you release those parts of your identity that no longer serve you, it can be an emotionally uncomfortable or even painful process. It can feel as though parts of you are dying—which indeed they are. It's important to have adequate support as you dismantle your old identity. You may also want to join a spiritual community. That group can provide a safe place for you to explore the unknown on your journey. Fellow spiritual travelers can be there for you on a regular and long-term basis. A spiritual community can provide an external context of safety when you encounter internal places that may not always feel safe.

In this process you will be dismantling the parts of you that no longer serve your highest truth. You will be focusing on those inner structures you are ready to let go of. They include outdated belief systems, unresolved emotional wounds, and old survival mechanisms. You will also concentrate on your true essence—the unchanging source of love that you already are. It is a process of shifting your attention back and forth on these two aspects until, over time, your new identity, as pure love, stabilizes. In other words, you will need to face your inner blocks, the barriers to your inner source of love, in order to dissolve them. Those barriers have been blocking your view—your inner light, your true essence.

The Ultimate Observer

As we come to remember and to know the highest truth of who we are, we experience ourselves as the ultimate observer of all things. In meditation, we no longer identify with or try to control our mind. Rather we simply bring our awareness to that truest part of ourselves, the energy field of our inner essence. As love, we witness all things in our life through the eyes of compassion and understanding. When we truly know ourselves to be love, to be peace, we recognize in ourselves the very qualities that we have assigned to God. Knowing ourselves *as* those qualities allows us to *be* that in the world. We no longer need to wait or expect somebody else to demonstrate those qualities in our lives. We *become* the model of it, demonstrating to others the possibility of living in peace and harmony, here and now. No waiting is required. We become a living example to others that it is safe to live openheartedly, *as* love, in this world.

At this mystical level of living, there is no longer any desire or need to blame, judge, or to make others wrong. And if we do momentarily forget who we are, we can easily find our way back to *being* love. We understand and have compassion for the human condition. We see that the vast majority of people are still trapped in a limited, separate identity. They have forgotten their true nature. They are a potential danger to themselves and to others. Coming from a place of separation and fear, they believe they live in a dangerous world. When their safety feels threatened, they are convinced there is no alternative but to attack others in order to preserve their well-being. This way of being currently plagues humanity. The biblical phrase—*"Forgive them, for they know not what they have done"*—comes to mind. How could they know, when they have assumed a false identity?

Living Beyond Our Stories

From the highest viewpoint, forgiving others is natural because we can readily admit that whatever "wrong" another might have committed, we have committed the same or a similar wrong ourselves—even if only in our imagination. We know their so-called wrong was the result of ignorance, born out of fear, as a result of their forgotten identity. The ultimate forgiveness is to have compassion toward those who taught us false ideas from an old paradigm of separation, in the first place. We understand they were taught the same things by those who came before them. They had also forgotten their true identity, which is love. At the mystical level of awareness, we recognize there is actually nothing *to* forgive, ever. We see that all there is to do is simply return to the truth, and move beyond the belief or appearance of a separate self.

It is also possible that we have held a grudge against someone for something that never actually happened, at least not in the way we believed. I realized this in my 20s, when I was examining painful incidents of my past in order to resolve what still seemed unhealed. I remember calling my two sisters to have them corroborate the details of certain childhood happenings. To my surprise, they both recounted different versions of the same events, which seemed equally true for each of them. It occurred to me that the three of us had three different, yet equally real, experiences of the same occurrences, the same childhood. We all had different childhoods, and therefore we have created different "stories" about ourselves and the world at large.

With clear vision, we see that it no longer serves us to cling to *any* story of wrongdoing, either by oneself or by another. What would be the benefit of continuing to perpetuate stories that are not in alignment with the truth that we are *all* essentially love? The fact that most of us are still living in a state of forgetfulness of that fundamental truth doesn't change that reality. As we shift our perspective about who and what we truly are, that in turn shifts the nature of the world we inhabit and our experience of others. The world becomes a more loving place because *we* have become a more loving, openhearted human being. And all we did was come into alignment with what was already true. This is what it means to live beyond our stories—about ourselves, others, and the world.

The Shortcut

The Truth—that we are all essentially pure love—is actually quite simple. Our minds often want a more complicated reality. Many of the great spiritual leaders and teachers are in agreement that, as human beings, we have merely forgotten our true identity. We have been misled into a world of illusion by the teachings and beliefs of others who have also forgotten who they are.

What obscures the realization of who and what we truly are? Any thought, belief, or experience that does not affirm that we are love. We need to question anything or anyone who would tell us otherwise. In the end, the only practice needed is one that points us back to this truth. And it can be as simple as finding the willingness to be fully present with whatever is happening, at any given moment. As the observer, we allow life to be exactly as it is. We can safely let go of resisting or trying to change or fix things, including ourselves. From this place of inner spaciousness and inner stillness, useful action naturally emerges. When we no longer feel a need or desire to control anything or anybody, the useful action becomes obvious. It is organically made known to us, from within. Proper action is always in alignment with the highest good for the whole. It naturally facilitates the shifting of consciousness in the direction of awakening. This enables us to operate from the mystical level of awareness. This is the only way that true and lasting change can emerge on this planet.

As our vision clears, it becomes obvious that any understanding *other* than knowing oneself to be love just does not make sense. Anything else is insane, because it leads to insane behavior. It creates division and conflict and eventually leads to war, to all kinds of abuse of people, animals, and the earth itself. It leads to untold suffering. This has reached such an extreme that our very survival is currently under threat. Is this not insanity? The only way to create a functional, harmonious, loving humanity and world is simply to remember ourselves to *be* love. It is our true nature, and we need to let our actions be in alignment with that knowing.

Our mind might want to believe there is one particular way to achieve this. However, many different paths and practices can take us in a useful direction. They can provide us with tools to deconstruct our outdated beliefs and habits. In the end, though, it might be as simple as choosing to be a loving human being. We simply let go of whatever stands in the way of that. Remember, that's what we already are.

Being love in this world may occasionally leave us feeling vulnerable. It requires laying down all of our defenses. There is a certain gentleness, a harmlessness that emanates from those who have truly awakened to their authentic nature. For when we deeply knows ourselves to be love, this is the ultimate safety. Nothing and nobody can harm pure love. It is both harmless and unharmable. Unconditional love is unbreakable. Knowing ourselves to be love means that we are in touch with an inner, reliable feeling of safety. We know we can trust our inner knowing at any given moment, whatever the situation. Being love means that we are keenly tuned into our inner guidance or direction. When we trust it enough we are also willing to act on it.

A Deeper Look at Self-Love

Many, if not all of us, grew up with a somewhat damaged sense of self. Childhood hurts, traumas, or abuse severely distorted our self-image and it can interfere with our ability to relate to others in healthy ways. If this is the case for you, it is important to do the emotional healing work to resolve whatever is still affecting you from the past. On your journey of healing, you need to develop unconditional acceptance and compassion for your wounded inner child. You need to be aware if you are acting out and/or demanding your needs be met by others who may not be capable of, or willing to meet them. Loving the wounded parts of yourself is a vital step in creating a healthy ego in order to have functional relationships.

However, as we move into the mystical level of consciousness, and we fully know ourselves to *be* love, we recognize there is actually no separate self *to* love. The very idea of loving oneself suggests duality, where in fact, there is only oneness. Self-love implies that we are separate from the source of love, rather than an expression of it. From the highest level of truth, the greatest act of "self-love" is to truly know who and what we are. Love is the truth of who we are. When we truly know this, everything changes. Can it be that simple? I say yes!

Chapter Nine

TRUE ABUNDANCE

*"Nature is neither pleasant nor painful. It is all intelligence
and beauty. Pain and pleasure are in the mind. Change
your scale of values and all will change. Pleasure and pain
are mere disturbances of the senses; treat them equally and
there will be only bliss. The world is what you make it;
by all means make it happy. Only contentment can make
you happy; desires fulfilled breed more desires. Keeping
away from all desires, and contentment with what comes
by itself, is a very fruitful state, a precondition to the
state of fullness. Don't distrust its apparent sterility and
emptiness. Believe me, it is the satisfaction of desires that
breeds misery. Freedom from desires is bliss."*
— *Sri Nisargadatta Maharaj*

Forgiveness

Why start the conversation about abundance with forgiveness?
Forgiveness allows us to be fully present in this moment, right
here, right now. Forgiveness enables us to wholeheartedly embrace
what is and to be at peace with our past and fully engaged with the
present. Making peace with our past is the most immediate way
we can experience the abundance that is our birthright. Without
forgiveness—of ourselves and others—there is always something

pulling us out of alignment with ourselves and with life; it is an energy drain in our system. Until we have made perfect peace with all that has occurred in our life, and with all the people who have played a part in it, we deny ourselves the full richness of our true abundance. Forgiveness is a gift we give to ourselves. It frees up the energy we had invested in making another, or ourselves, "wrong." Ultimately, forgiveness is letting go of the illusion that something actually ever went wrong.

Many of us put the onus of forgiveness on God. Although I didn't grow up in a religious household, early in life, I adopted the idea that God is an external entity. My personal understanding of God has gone through many evolutions over the years. My present perception is God as *energy*, not *entity*. I like to say that I no longer have a "God with skin." And if God is energy, how can it forgive? Forgiveness implies judgment. There's no judgment in energy.

The human mind is constantly judging. The human mind labels virtually everything it encounters as "good or bad," or "right or wrong," or "light or dark." In doing this, it creates the illusion of separation. But the human mind is not God Mind. And we, as humans, are not solely our minds. I believe the rightful purpose of the human mind is to serve divine mind, which is synonymous with love. This mind ultimately *is* all.

How do we forge a connection between our human mind and divine mind? The best way is by being in *the silence*. Although we can make the connection in various ways, the most immediate and direct way is in meditation. In the silence of meditation, when we are truly present with life exactly as it is, without any resistance, our mind is finally able to find peace. In silence, we are able to let go of limited human concepts and experience an expanded state of awareness. In this infinite awareness there is nothing to change and nothing to try to manifest. We feel a deep knowing that we are perfect expressions of the totality. And ultimately we know ourselves *as* that, with no separation. *This is true abundance.*

Getting It Right

In the early 1990s I traveled to India and visited the ashram of Amma (Sri Mata Amritanandamayi Devi), who is also known as the "hugging guru." It was a truly amazing experience to be in her presence. I experienced her to be pure light, pure love, and pure essence. It was as though there was nothing left of her but joy and gratitude. Often a beautiful, childlike laughter would bubble up from within her. However, one thing that stood out was how everybody around her was trying hard to "follow the rules" and "do it right." Here I sensed a kind of rigidity, which was in sharp contrast to her gentle, loving, presence. Her followers seemed to believe that if they sat in the right place, in the correct position, or stood with the proper posture, and said the right thing, that that would greatly contribute to their spiritual awakening.

Somehow, this felt like the antithesis of spiritual awakening to me. And I strongly doubted that Amma concerned herself about how her devotees were sitting. There is a widely held belief in many spiritual circles that "if I can just learn to pray or meditate in exactly the 'right' way, then one day I too will be like the enlightened teacher." But what if we don't need to do anything perfectly? What if we don't need to do anything other than just be who we naturally are? What if it is OK to just be ourselves, without any pretenses? What if there is nothing for us to strive for or to become other than a fully authentic expression of our unique selves? I have come to the conclusion that there is actually no "there" to get to—because the abundant life we seek is *already here.* Most of us just have not yet recognized it.

The important question for me has become: "How can I shift my perspective of *what is,* in this moment, so that I can be at peace with it, just as it is, rather than trying to fix or change it?" There was a time when I strongly believed that if only I could "do it right"—go to the right workshops, find the right job, or meet the right partner—that somehow everything would be OK. And that *I* would be OK. I was not able to see that my abundance was *already here.* All I needed to do was let go of my concepts and ideas of how things "should" be different. In retrospect, all that needed to actually happen was for me to loosen the grip of my judgments regarding myself, and the world.

Yoga has become popular in recent years. As a spiritual practice from India, yoga is essentially about the inward journey. It is a path or vehicle that enables us to find our inner alignment with source. It is a way to bring awareness to the places where there is spiritual or physical resistance. We find out what happens when we hold a pose for a moment longer, leaning into our discomfort. It is an excellent metaphor for our spiritual lives. Discovering where we are resisting and unwilling to move toward discomfort. However, here in the United States, yoga has become a technique and a measure of achievement. We are into "power yoga" and comparing and competing. I recently heard that yoga might become an Olympic sport. How would judges measure yoga, as a competitive sport? Would it be "This person is more at one with source than that person over here"? More likely, contestants would be judged by how perfect the asana or pose appears, from the outside, or how long a person can hold a pose. "Her ankle needs to be one degree over to the right," or "He wins because he held the pose for 30 seconds longer."

Although this sounds a bit absurd, it is a good analogy for what I used to believe spirituality was all about. I once thought that I could measure my success by how much I had managed to manifest in my outer life. I judged spiritual "success" on whether I had obtained the things I wanted. This now seems equally absurd to me. I have come to realize that true abundance is about *inner alignment with source*. It is about knowing who and what we truly are, in our connection and oneness with source and therefore, knowing our connectedness and oneness with the whole of life.

Prosperity or Abundance?

"Prosperity" used to be a trigger word for me in the same way that the word "God" triggers a reaction in some people. A great example of this is how my nephew Orion, who was six years old at the time, came to me with questions about God. I was faced with the challenge of sharing my understandings with him, without telling him what I think he "should" believe. Anyone who is a parent or caretaker of a child can probably relate to this. I felt it was important that he have his own inner journey and discovery of his relationship with God. I didn't want to influence him too much. Like the word God, prosperity may conjure up a particular meaning for you. Quite often people equate it with material or financial success.

In my pursuit of happiness and the *inner feeling* of abundance, I found myself, like most people, chasing after material goals. I had learned in one incarnation of my spiritual training that "thoughts held in mind produce after their kind." I understood this to mean that if I affirmed the things that I wanted to manifest, and held them in my mind, in the "right" way, that I would draw them to me. This in turn would bring me happiness and a feeling of abundance. In fact, I believed that if I were truly living a "spiritual life" then I should be able to manifest all the things I wanted. The results would indicate how well I was doing.

What I discovered, though, was that by using these Law of Attraction principles, I could indeed manifest the things I wanted.

I created a successful business that enabled me to live the lifestyle I thought I needed to be happy and fulfilled. But guess what? After achieving all the external trappings, I did not feel the satisfaction I had anticipated. In fact, the opposite was true. I felt increasingly emptier inside. And I wanted more things to fill that emptiness. Emotionally and spiritually, I did not feel the abundance I had been searching for. My thinking and actions became distorted, which eventually led me to cause harm to myself and others. Selfishness and the need to fill the inner emptiness ruled my life. The trajectory of my life gradually took me to a very dark and lonely place. I was riddled with guilt, blame, and shame about the harm I had caused others, and I became depressed and despondent. Then things in my outer life started falling apart, and I ended up losing everything. I got to see how attached I had become to what I had accumulated and how my level of consciousness had created quite a mess.

That dark period lasted for nearly a year. Through meditation, self-inquiry, support from a loving spiritual community, and simply learning to be with these difficult feelings and experiences, I eventually had a profound and intense spiritual awakening. I was able to redirect my attention from "getting what I wanted" and place it firmly on my inner alignment. My alignment was with my true purpose in this life, and with the truth of who I really am. It was after that experience that I dedicated my life to helping others and serving the new paradigm of consciousness. My life would never be the same. I quite literally felt like I had been reborn.

The Seduction of the Ego

Jim Carrey said: *"I think everybody should get rich and famous and do everything they ever dreamed of so they can see that it's not the answer."* Although it was difficult and heartbreaking at the time, I am now able to look back and see the gift in those challenging events in my life. I can see how making material manifestation my sole aim caused me to lose touch with my soul's aim. But paradoxically, when I pursued outer wealth, it eventually led me, in a roundabout way, to aligning with my true purpose. My losses caused me to turn back within. I had to dig deeper inside myself for the feeling of abundance I was seeking. It ultimately led me to the discovery that *my life was already inherently abundant. I did not need to add anything to it.* And that *I was already perfect, just as I was.*

I know this divine perfection to exist at the core of all of us, and at the core of all of life. It is our true essence. For most of us, it has been buried under layers and layers of illusion and false ideas about who we are. The spiritual journey is one of uncovering perceived obstacles and unearthing the truth of who we are, rather than adding anything to ourselves. Instead of affirming what I want, I now affirm the truth of the oneness that already is. I trust that life responds accordingly. Please do not misunderstand me. There is absolutely nothing wrong with going after material things or enjoying a financially prosperous existence. However, we need to understand that nothing outside is going to provide us with lasting satisfaction. If we believe that acquiring something is going to make us feel complete, then we are living in an illusion. External wealth or objects at best give us a temporary feeling of abundance or happiness. It is our connection with our inner source which provides permanent abundance in our lives.

Manifestation is life's natural, automatic response to who I am *being.* Life cannot help but manifest all around me, in accordance with my state of being, my state of consciousness. And if I am *being abundance*—because I am attuned to source—that is what will naturally manifest in my personal life. Living in this way, there is nothing to chase, and nothing to attain. Rather, the door is opened to living in a state of grace and of harmony with the whole of life.

There is also a natural desire to share this inner richness with those around me. *I don't attract what I want, I attract what I am.*

Look Back but Don't Stare

I have spent much of my life looking back and staring at the past and its events. It has been an attempt to figure out what really happened in my life and why. Looking back is helpful up to a certain point. But, once we have learned what we needed to learn, we can safely release the past, making ourselves fully available for the present moment. We might have told certain stories about ourselves: "I'm not good enough"… "I'm not capable of …" We can put those stories to rest. In doing so we can become who we were born to be. We find the freedom to choose who we want to be and how we want to live, rather than letting the past continue to dictate it to us.

Security

For people living in the United States, which places a high priority on outer achievement, it seems natural to make outer goals a personal priority. A recent survey revealed that the number one thing that is important to Americans is security. It is simply the way each of us perceives what security is that creates our desires and possible attachments. For example, for some, security might be amassing more guns. For others of us, it might be getting rid of them altogether. In the same way, our national obsession to acquire more and more material wealth may be rooted in this deep desire for security.

These days, with outer structures becoming less stable, there is evidence that external things are not a reliable measurement of security. But what is security, really? We are discovering that it is not in our 401K, or in buying more insurance. It's not in finding the "right" job or having the perfect partner. What is left when the next 8.0 earthquake hits (in reality or symbolically) and we no longer have what we thought was ours to keep? True security is found when we have made a firm connection with the bedrock of our being. It is the *only true source of security, within.* Until then we will never feel truly secure in this rapidly changing world.

Divine Integration

One of my favorite authors is Pema Chodron. She describes beautifully how we can *be with* our experience, whatever that might be. In her words: "*We are told from childhood that something is wrong with us, with the world, and with everything that comes along. It is not perfect. It has rough edges. It has a bitter taste. It's too loud, too soft. Too sharp, too wishy-washy. We cultivate a sense of trying to make things better because something is bad here. Something is a mistake here. Something is a problem here. The main point of spiritual teaching is to dissolve the dualistic struggle against what is happening to us. These teachings instruct us to move toward difficulties rather than backing away. We don't get this kind of encouragement very often. Everything that occurs is not only useable and workable, it actually is the path itself. We can use everything that happens to us as a means for waking up. We can use everything that occurs, whether it is conflicting emotions and thoughts, or our seemingly outer situation, to show us where we are asleep. And how we can wake up completely, utterly, without reservations.*"

We are so used to dividing our world and our experiences into what we deem as spiritual and what we deem to be human. But these arbitrary judgments do not mean much at all when we are able to view life through the lens of oneness. In fact, these divisions are only real inside our minds, creating artificial walls of separation between ourselves and the world around us. Without them, we are able to step into a whole new world where there is the possibility of seeing the perfection of each and every moment. This is a life of radical acceptance of what is.

Perhaps the deepest meaning of abundance is the absolute knowing our *internal* oneness. It is the integration of those parts within us we might call *human* and those parts we see as *spirit*. With this knowledge, we automatically live a life of abundance regardless of outer circumstances. And, of course, when we truly understand that, all is well with us and with the world. This is living a life of true abundance.

Chapter Ten

SHIFT HAPPENS

"I've found that every spiritual advance I've made was preceded by some sort of fall—in fact, it's almost a universal law that a fall of some kind precedes a major shift. An accident, a fire that destroys all the stuff we've worked so hard to accumulate, an illness, a failed relationship, a death or injury that causes deep sorrow, an abandonment, a serious addiction, a business failure, a bankruptcy, or the like. These low points actually provide the energy needed to make a shift in the direction away from an ego-driven life to one full of purpose."
— *Excerpt from* The Shift, *by Dr. Wayne Dyer*

Reframing

The original version of the phrase, of course, is "shit happens" which refers to the fact that, from time to time, we all face things in life that we would rather not experience. Sometimes we experience moments of loss, pain, destruction, and life not unfolding as we would prefer it to. In the old paradigm, life's experiences are seen as either "good or bad." We embrace the good, and reject the bad. But this creates a dualistic world. What if we reframed the original phrase and said "fertilizer" rather than "shit"? When seen in that light, not only is the so-called "bad" helpful, but it actually has value. Fertilizer is a naturally occurring element in the cycle of organic life that feeds and contributes to the growth of the next cycle. Nature's intelligence makes use of everything that is available to it. Fertilizer happens.

When we choose to similarly reframe our thinking about the unwanted or undesirable events in our lives, they too can become valuable. What if, in the bigger picture, everything we experience—no matter how we feel about it—contributes toward our growth? What if we stopped resisting and judging anything or anybody as "wrong" or "bad"? Perhaps the wrong or bad could have a fertilizing effect on us. We don't need to divide life into whom or what is for us and whom or what is against us. With a small, but profound, shift in perspective, we can step into a world where *absolutely everything* is useful. And then we can decide that the negative is happening *for* us. In this way, we can create a world where there is no wrong, no mistakes, and no enemies.

This world of "nothing is against me" is, indeed, the world that those who are spiritually awake inhabit. *Nothing in the external world needs to change in order for us to live in this new paradigm.* In this new world, we are still free to choose how we interpret our experiences. Every moment is an opportunity to remain open and connected, or to close off and reject. Each experience in our daily life is an opportunity to respond by *being* love. The alternative is to allow fear to dominate our existence.

It is important to recognize that the old paradigm has been our stepping stone. It enabled us to reach the point where we are now ready to take a leap in consciousness. Rather than rejecting our old ways by making them wrong, we can acknowledge the path we have taken that has brought us to where we are now. Having understanding and compassion for our old conditioning, habits, and belief systems eases our passage into the new. Seeing the value in where we have come from enables us to accept our past with gratitude. In fact, this is the only mind-set that allows us to enter and remain in the new paradigm of wholeness. In a paradigm of wholeness, everything has its place. Nothing is excluded.

Making U-turns

When our life, or an aspect of it, appears not to be working, it might seem like it is time for us to make a U-turn. When things are falling apart, or we find ourselves facing a major roadblock or difficulty, more often than not, making a U-turn is the most effective next step. When we make a U-turn, we turn and look in the opposite direction. Perhaps we are just not feeling the joy or satisfaction we know is possible. Sometimes the solution we seek eludes us. Our tendency is to look outside ourselves for answers, for solutions, and satisfaction. Perhaps the answer is not about anything needing to change on the outside. The U-turn in which I am referring is a turn from an outer-focused life to an inner-focused way of being.

Here in the USA, we live primarily in an outward-focused culture. We believe that everything we want and need is "out there." Notice how much money our government has spent on space exploration, but we know little of life at the bottom of the ocean. This serves as a great metaphor. When we cannot find what we are seeking, it might be because we are looking for it in a place where it cannot be found. When we make a U-turn, we turn within, and tap into a different method of knowing. By looking within, we tune into a network of inner communication where we have access to information that is not available to us when we are only focused outward. By turning within, a new clarity becomes available. That is because we are now facing the direction of source, from which everything flows. By making a U-turn, we have more direct access to finding out what is true for us.

Sometimes it takes another person to point us within. They can provide a listening field that allows us to travel inwardly and connect with our truth. A close friend or a healing professional— perhaps a therapist or a spiritual guide—can give us deep, uninterrupted listening. Such a situation can create the focused stillness we need in order to hear our thoughts, and discover our innate knowing.

Trusting Our Inner Guide

A number of years ago, I was earning my living by waiting tables at a restaurant. One evening, while working in the restaurant, I had a conversation with a close friend. He asked, "So, what's going on for you? Is waiting tables working for you? Is that what you want to be doing?" In that moment, it really struck me that I no longer felt that I was living my purpose. My friend's direct questions caused me to take an honest look within and to consider how I was spending my working hours. Two years previously, my life had felt very much "on purpose." At that time, I was employed as a counselor in a residential treatment facility for people in early recovery from chemical addiction. I loved that work and desperately wanted to return to it. My friend's questions pointed me inward to find my truth. My desire to return to counseling suddenly became very clear to me. I had a powerful inner "click." Within days of this conversation and my new awareness of my inner calling, my life dramatically changed. I had seen my friend on a Tuesday. That same evening, I was moved to take a leap of faith and gave my two-week notice at the restaurant without a "safety net." The very next day, another friend invited me to a luncheon where he was giving a speech. Remarkably, the luncheon was to take place at a residential treatment center, at which my friend was an alumni.

I accepted the invitation and, at that event, I met some of the treatment program directors. They invited me to another luncheon which was happening the following week. It was there that I learned about an available position. I immediately applied for the open job. After they read my resume, I was offered a first, and then a second interview. During the second interview, the program director looked at me and said, "This position isn't quite right for you. I think we need to create one that would be a better fit. What would you create for yourself if you could do anything you wanted?" I was able to articulate exactly what I wanted to create. He consequently hired me to develop and implement a spiritual care program and serve as the spiritual care counselor. It was perfectly tailored to suit my skills and interests. Within a miraculously short period of time, I found myself working at my dream job, and feeling very much back on purpose.

A Shift from Ego to Spirit

One of my responsibilities at the treatment center was to provide spiritual counseling to clients in their first week of treatment. The new arrivals were all going through a painful and confusing time in their lives. As I sat with them I was reminded that my truest purpose was to simply see them clearly—for whom they really were, beneath their external appearances. My highest priority was to see them as their inner essence—pure love and pure light. I became fully present with each and every client. It was an extremely transformational experience—both for the client and for me. I discovered that when I saw them *as* their innate spiritual essence— rather than as their outward or ego identity—I also became free of my ego identity. As I shifted my focus on how I viewed others, my attachment to my ego identity shifted. I saw that essence can only be truly seen and recognized by essence. When we develop this ability to see through and beyond the ego, we are freed to experience the purity of our spiritual essence, beyond our ego. All that is required is the willingness to shift our focus of attention from ego to spirit.

Working in the treatment facility, I had numerous opportunities to make this shift of focus. Sometimes a client would start acting out and screaming, "Oh my God, oh my God, I need to get out of this place!" When that happened I recognized it as an opportunity to shift my focus. I learned to see beyond that person's ego. I perceived someone who was frightened, maybe terrified, to receive the love and care that was available to them in that moment. The client was most likely unaware of why they were feeling what they were feeling. One client started yelling, "They won't give me my hairdryer! I need my hairdryer!" While I understood their emotional reaction *seemed* to be about not getting to use a hairdryer, I was also aware that the hairdryer was not the true cause of their distress. I also understood their distrust and honored they felt a lack of safety. They might have calmed down if they had the hairdryer, but the root of their upset went much deeper than that.

When we can simply *be* in the presence of whoever is in front of us, it becomes clear that any display of bizarre behavior is actually a request for love. And underneath that, there is a deep-seated fear of being fully present with what is. Those who have struggled with addiction know how it feels to spend their life running away from simply being present with themselves. As humans, we find so many different ways to escape. Addictions, and all kinds of compulsive behaviors and habits, are always an attempt to run away from ourselves and from what we are experiencing, in the moment.

When I make it my highest priority to simply honor the presence of a client, miraculous shifts happen. They do not really need me to *do* anything in particular. I just need to be fully present with them, and to see them for who they really are. Giving a client the experience of being truly seen—beyond their physical appearance and ego identity—opens the door for transformation to happen. If they are seen as a clinical diagnosis or as someone with a mental illness, that is how they will view and experience themselves. When I simply witness their innate spiritual essence, the possibility of their own self-realization becomes much more available.

Everything Is Love or a Request for Love

You may be familiar with the idea that everything—all thoughts, words, and behavior—is rooted in either love or fear. Although this idea has been a useful one for me, my awareness has shifted to a new understanding—that *everything is love or a request for love*. My work in the addiction treatment field teaches me that underneath all the strange and sometimes hostile behaviors, at the root there is always a request for love. Sometimes, as human beings, we simply do not know how to ask for what we need or want. We lose touch with the truth of our being. When I look back at my own life, I see that the times of addiction and seemingly crazy behavior were simply my way of seeking love. It was the only way I knew how, at that time, to seek the feeling of safety and wholeness, which I believed were lacking.

Time in the Wilderness

Before making a major shift, we often go through a period of being "lost in the wilderness." We are unable to find our way forward.

Maybe we are confused and do not know which direction to proceed. Or we experience a major loss of something that held enormous value to us. Or someone, who we thought we couldn't live without, is suddenly gone. These times are comparable to the "40 days and nights in the wilderness," from Christian teachings, and whether you celebrate Christian traditions or not, the metaphor can be a very useful one. According to the Bible, Jesus' time in the wilderness was followed by his crucifixion, and subsequent burial and resurrection. Lent—the period of time preceding Easter—is generally acknowledged by fasting or giving up a habit. The abstinence symbolizes the release of an old way of doing things or an old state of being. It is sometimes interpreted as a time in which it is "noble" to suffer. The period of Lent and the symbolic death of the old is always followed by the celebration of new life, the resurrection.

This religious tradition is an accurate metaphor for the natural cycles of life. We know full well that a resurrection will follow an experience such as "being in the wilderness" and the "crucifixion." It is also important for us to recognize and honor where we are at, in any given cycle of our life, at any given moment. We need to be totally honest with ourselves and allow the full experience of being in the darkness. It can generate the energy to carry us forward into the birth of a new cycle. In this way, it is not helpful to dismiss or deny the uncomfortable parts of our lives.

In New Thought teachings there has been a tendency to gloss over the "wilderness experience." Many want to immediately put their attention on what makes them feel better. And in the midst of a dark night of the soul, nobody wants to be told, "You'll get over it" or "Not to worry, things are bound to get better." Although it's certainly true that things will get better, given time, it's not in the least bit helpful to deny what one is feeling, when one is in pain or suffering. As my friend Rev. Sonya Milton sometimes says, *"Nothing could be truer, and less helpful."* Acknowledging and including the darkness of our experience allows us to own our wholeness.

As stated in the quote at the beginning of this chapter, Dr. Wayne Dyer says that some kind of fall always precedes every major spiritual advance. It's nature's way of moving things forward. By allowing ourselves to open our hearts to whatever we are feeling we reorient ourselves away from our ego-driven need to control our experience. We can then move in the direction of deeper meaning and purpose. When life forces us to surrender our control, we are gifted the opportunity to expand and deepen our heart's capacity to feel. Surrendering makes it possible for us to reach new heights of emotional and spiritual upliftment that will inevitably follow.

Acceptance and Denial

It is one thing to fully acknowledge, accept, and feel what is difficult in our lives. When we do that—consciously choosing to move our thinking to a new place that will uplift or comfort us—we find inner peace and harmony about a given situation. But it's another thing to be in denial of what is happening. We need to overcome fear and let ourselves visit the darker inner places.

When our house is burning down, it makes no sense to pretend that it's not happening. It's perfectly natural to want to protect ourselves from pain. It takes courage to remain openhearted, even in the midst of our greatest challenges. Facing our difficulties allows us to experience even greater expansion of mind, heart, and spirit. Suffering is always rooted in our attachment to have things be a certain way. We believe that if we had total control over our circumstances, we would possess the key to our happiness. But the truth is; happiness is *always* available to us, in every moment, *no matter how our circumstances look*. We can always find a purpose for whatever life presents us. In reality, there is nothing to be sought, or found. Nobody needs to be saved. All that we seek is absolutely available to us, in this moment. When we turn within, and remember our oneness with source, we know we are complete.

There is an amusing story in the New Thought movement about two ministers who are visiting San Francisco. They park their car at the top of one of the city's famous steep hills. Being new to the city, they fail to engage the hand brake and to curb the tires of their car. As they are walking away, the car begins to roll down the hill, sideswiping every vehicle in its path and finally crashing into a cable car. On seeing the catastrophic damage, one of the ministers turns to the other and joyfully says, "Well, I just can't wait to see the good that is going to come from this!"

The Shift Is Internal

Certain events have been strongly associated with the shifting of human consciousness. Many references have been made, since the 1960s, to the coming Age of Aquarius. Another one of those events was the lineup of planets known as the Harmonic Convergence in August 1987. And a more recent example was the "Mayan Apocalypse," which was predicted for December 21, 2012. These historical and astrological moments are certainly significant, and are no doubt relevant to transforming human consciousness. But the shift I am speaking of is not about an external event or a change in external reality. It's about a shift in *the way we view* external reality. It's a shift in our relationship with ourselves and with the external world. The shift is one from outer focus to inner knowing.

The shift is one that requires cleaning the lens through which we see life, others, and ourselves.

Inner shifts can occur in small, almost imperceptible increments. Or they can happen as more noticeable changes that organically occur within us. Every moment holds the possibility of a deeper awakening to the truth of who we are. Inner shifting is an ongoing process that happens over time, as consciousness awakens to itself. Or, it can happen in a moment of profound awakening. Everybody's path is unique. Teachers, books, philosophies, religions can all point us toward the truth, but in the end, truth is something to be discovered within oneself. The truth that we seek is not a destination, but rather, it is *who and what we are.*

Chapter Eleven

AN EVER-CHANGING WORLD

"It's extremely important to investigate the causes and origins of suffering; how it arises. One must begin that process by appreciating the impermanent, transient nature of our existence. All things, events, and phenomena are dynamic, changing in every moment; nothing remains static. And since all things are subject to change, nothing exists in a permanent condition; nothing is able to remain the same under its own independent power. Thus, all things are under the influence of other factors. So, at any given moment, no matter how pleasant or pleasurable your experience may be, it will not last. This becomes the basis of a category of suffering known in Buddhism as the 'suffering of change.'"

— The Dalai Lama

Embracing Change

Resistance to change is a natural human tendency. Our egoic mind identity constantly seeks to preserve itself, and the status quo, in order to feel safe and secure. Despite so much evidence to the contrary, most of us cling to the belief that our safety and security are to be found in the external world. By its very nature, the physical world is in a constant state of change. Life is dynamic. Nothing remains static for long. As human beings, we tend to resist this natural forward movement of life. But the impermanence of things is not something we should learn to begrudgingly accept. Rather, we can understand that it's one of life's greatest gifts. Without change, life becomes frozen, leaving no possibility for improvement and growth. If nothing changes, then nothing changes. Without evolutionary change, we would still be living in caves, and making fire by rubbing two sticks together.

As I shared in a previous chapter, there was a time in my life when my entire personal outer world collapsed. One of the unexpected gifts I received as a result of those losses was that the unchanging aspect of myself became profoundly highlighted. My awareness of the eternal truth within me was awakened. As I learned to live my life rooted in this inner changeless place, I no longer felt a need to cling to external things for a sense of stability. I no longer felt tossed around by life's ups and downs. Instead, I felt grounded in the eternality of spirit. With this shift of identity to the invisible dimension of my life, there was a new lightness of being and a willingness to flow with the outer changes that were naturally occurring. I could enjoy what I was experiencing at any given moment. I had less desire to hold onto it or make it permanent. I was in touch with a sense of inner safety, in this ever-changing world.

This inner safety is not dependent on any external thing whatsoever. It comes from knowing who we truly are and being grounded in spirit. It doesn't guarantee us physical safety, or emotional safety. There are many who want to maintain these kinds of safety at all costs. Yet people who remain safe rarely change the world. And, we are all here changing the world, simply by serving the new paradigm. We are here to change our *own* world, and the eyes through which we view it. Paradoxically, it is our willingness to embrace our feelings of lack of external safety and insecurity that allows us to transition to the next level of consciousness. By releasing our grip on what was, we let an old aspect of ourselves die—a belief, an attachment—creating space for the new awareness to be born and emerge. When we trust the naturally occurring movements of life, we can release feelings of stress and worries about the future. We let go of any circumstances that are disintegrating. We willingly embrace the new ones that are integrating. In times of change, there may well be moments when our ego feels frightened and wants to resist, but our spirit remains forever courageous.

The phrase "survival of the fittest" has been associated with Charles Darwin. However, his real point was that the species that are most capable of adapting to change are the ones that survive. He said: *"It is not the strongest or the most intelligent who will survive but those who can best manage change."* When we no longer identify with the changing externals of our lives, but see the unchanging spirit within, we have a stable foundation from which to witness the constant movement of our lives. No matter what changes, we— as the witness—do not. We are then free to adapt to outer change without clinging and attaching. Like the thrill of a roller coaster ride, we can feel exhilaration, rather than anxiety and fear, as we move through the changing scenes of our lives. And whether the changes are planned or if we are caught off guard by unexpected changes, we can trust that, in the larger scheme of things, all is well.

Pain and Suffering

Pain is part of the human experience. Naturally, most of us prefer to feel loved, safe, and connected, rather than sad, lonely, or afraid. But the latter feelings are unavoidable parts of being human. In Buddhism, the First Noble Truth states that: *"Pain in life is inevitable but suffering is not. Pain is what the world does to you, suffering is what you do to yourself. Pain is inevitable, suffering is optional.*" Suffering is optional because it is the result of how we deal with or process the experience of pain. Pain and pleasure are of the body, suffering is in the mind. One root cause of suffering is resisting pain and attaching to pleasure. Another is clinging to the idea that things in the external world need to look or be a certain way.

Pain is an internal navigational system, informing us that something needs our attention. If we resist or ignore the sounding of pain's guidance, we prolong it and create unnecessary suffering. In fact, when we resist anything that is happening in our internal *or* external experience, we create unnecessary suffering. When we refuse to let go of what no longer serves a purpose in our lives, clinging to what once was, we create unnecessary suffering.

Suffering ceases when we bring ourselves into full alignment with what is, trusting the unfolding of life in this moment. Suffering ceases when we stop resisting inevitable outer change. For, no matter what happens, we possess the creative power within us to pick ourselves up and continue in the direction of our heart's desires. Suffering ceases when we are willing to fully accept the whole gamut of our emotions, without judgment. For when we allow ourselves to fully feel what we feel, we understand that emotions exist as a wave of energy moving through us, and are temporary. Suffering ceases when we are willing to release what no longer serves us, even though it previously had purpose in our lives, knowing that life will bring us what we need, when we need it.

Loving or Changing?

Suffering ceases when we stop resisting who we naturally are. We are all beautiful, unique expressions of life. Several years ago, before moving into my apartment, I decided to paint it. I arrived at

9 A.M. one morning, with all of my painting supplies. At 11 P.M. the same day, I was still there, rolling out the paint, and feeling tired, hungry, and more than a bit shaky. It has always been my nature to keep going and going, pushing myself until I finish what needs to be done. On numerous occasions, I have found myself, at the end of a long day, feeling exactly the way I felt on this particular day. Because of this characteristic, I had always judged myself as being obsessive-compulsive. In countless ways, I was making myself "wrong." After that day of painting, I found myself berating myself, once more. My inner dialogue was: *"Oh my, here I am, doing this again....What on earth is wrong with me?"*

And then it hit me. *The spiritual path isn't about changing myself. It's about loving myself.* My inner dialogue shifted to: *"Well, perhaps this trait of mine is actually OK. Maybe my tendency to drive myself so hard is actually a gift, rather than a problem to be fixed. What I've been labeling as 'obsessive' all of my life might be viewed as 'highly energized or motivated' by another person."* It certainly feels far more loving to accept my natural way of doing things, than to make them wrong. If we want to have a happy existence, accepting and loving ourselves, just as we are, is important. And if we want to fully wake up to the truth of who and what we are, it's absolutely essential. In fact, the greatest gift we can offer to others and to ourselves is loving kindness. Paradoxically, the more we are able to love and accept ourselves, the more we can consciously choose what we want to change. When we no longer come from a perspective of guilt and shame, we are available to trust ourselves and come into a greater alignment with clear vision.

The spiritual journey is sometimes likened to making the ascent to the top of a mountain. From that higher perspective, one has a larger view of things. What did not make much sense from ground level makes more sense as one climbs higher. From the top of the mountain, all the pieces of the puzzle fit together, as one views the whole picture. Everything becomes crystal clear when it is seen from a distance. Although this is a helpful metaphor, I recently read something that suggested there is one problem with this imagery. The thought is that as we start climbing the mountain, we are leaving all those other people behind. And those poor people, still at the bottom of the mountain, aren't getting it. This idea, once again, creates the illusion of separation, of higher and lower. But nothing could be further from the truth.

Waking up to our true identity involves recognizing that every person we meet is an equal expression of the divine—whether they know it or not. Another person may or may not be conscious about the truth of who they truly are. However, if we are spiritually awake, we will have the capacity to see them as their true essence. A homeless person we pass on the street is an expression of the same source as ourselves. He or she deserves to be treated as such. There is a wonderful story that Ellen Burstyn tells about studying for a role. She dressed as a homeless person and took to the streets of Beverly Hills. She made a commitment to herself to eat only whatever was gifted to her that day. At one point, she approached two women having lunch at an outdoor table. As she walked toward the table, one of the women reached into her handbag, pulled out a $20 bill, and handed it to her. What was striking is she never looked at Ellen. She said that was a deeply painful moment and also a powerfully transformative moment, because she realized what is really important. Perhaps our desire to look down upon or ignore the disenfranchised is an indication of how we reject those parts of ourselves we view as negative or unhealed. Whatever enemy figure might still exist in our world is an expression of the same source as us (albeit perhaps an unconscious one). Treating anybody as less than that concretizes the ego.

When confronted with challenging people or situations that we find disagreeable or distasteful, the question is always: "What would love say, or do?" For in truth, there is only the divine, expressing itself uniquely through each body, mind, and heart. In choosing to see every person we encounter in that light, we give them the greatest gift possible—a reminder of their true identity. We provide a mirror of loving present-moment awareness in which they might see a reflection of who they truly are. And in these situations, we get to shine some light upon the people or situations that might potentially cause us to forget our own divinity.

Paradigm of Oneness

Our personal daily experience is constantly being shaped and colored by our internal dialogue. At any moment (especially when we are not feeling grounded), we might ask ourselves these questions: "What am I telling myself? What story am I presently creating and believing?" Our consciousness can only expand when we question what we believe to be true. If we want to move beyond our current limitations in any area of our lives, we need to be willing to question and let go of what we have considered to be real. Enlightenment becomes possible only when we have the courage to question *absolutely* everything we have believed to be true. Even the things we consider to be hard facts. Awakening to a new reality necessitates abandoning everything we have believed about ourselves and the world in which we live.

Just as people once believed the earth was the center of the universe, or that the earth was flat, we currently live in a paradigm where we believe in the reality of our separate existence. In this reality, it appears to be true that we need to struggle and strive—often just to survive. Living the life of our dreams, for the majority, is not even seen as a possibility. Even though it's true that each of us is a unique expression of life, quantum physics now reveals that we are all expressions of one field of existence. This field behaves like one mind. Science is proving what mystics have known for centuries—namely, that everything is connected and an expression of one life. We are each a hologram of that one field of life. We possess the same properties or qualities as our source. This is not complicated. It is very simple. Perhaps it is too simple for some highly developed minds to grasp.

Competition or Cooperation?

We've all been taught that "it's human nature to be competitive" and that "it's only human to be violent." In our Western culture, we hear these ideas from a young age. People are recognized and rewarded for their ability to compete. We award prizes and trophies to those who can do things better, faster, and smarter than others. It's how we measure success. Our national obsession with sports is all about who wins. We believe in the concept of "a winner and a loser." There is something disturbing to me about this way of thinking. In one version of reality, it's true that healthy competition causes us to strive to do our very best. It stretches the limits of what we think we are capable of.

I envision a world where we are all winners, where nobody loses. In response to this idea, someone recently said to me, "That's ridiculous! Somebody must win and somebody has to lose!" I wanted to ask them, "And how is that working out for you…or, for us?" How can we ever thrive as a species on this planet if for every winner, there is a loser? Are so many of us doomed to be losers, just because of the way we set it up in our minds? This will take a huge leap in consciousness. For many, this may not even seem possible, but magnificent new paradigms are often doubted by the masses before a major shift occurs.

If we look to nature as our teacher, we see an amazing and intricate web of cooperation. There is no competition just for the sake of competition. No species can exist independently of another species it depends upon for survival. Humanity is just beginning to comprehend the necessity to cooperate with nature, if it wants to continue to exist. Climate change is rapidly bringing this issue to the forefront of our consciousness. Because of our ignorance, humanity will need to cooperate with itself on a global scale in order to overcome the danger in which we now find ourselves. The human species can no longer be arrogant. It cannot exist independently from the well-being of the planet upon which it depends for its survival. It's time to shift from a stance of competition with nature and the planet to one of cooperation.

Our Unique Journeys

The spiritual journey is essentially the same for each of us. It's a journey of self-inquiry and discovering what is real, what is true. And yet the journey is an individualized one for every person who takes it. The world's religions and spiritual traditions might point us in the right direction and provide us with some preliminary steps. Nevertheless, at a certain point, we must all realize that we are essentially on our own unique path toward awakening. In order to fully individuate, we must let go of absolutely everything we have ever learned or believed to be true. We must trust our inner direction.

Changes in our personal lives are happening at warp speed. These days many of us feel compelled, as never before, to find inner stability. Not only is our external reality experiencing a rapid rate of change and renewal, but so are our inner worlds. (At the personality level) Our beliefs and perspectives need to disintegrate in order for new awareness to emerge. In relative reality, what was true for us 20 years ago is not necessarily true for us today, and no longer currently serves us *or* the whole of humanity. And what seems true for us today will no longer be our truth 20 years from now. It will take courage and faith to let go of these inner personality and egoic structures, which we had previously depended on for our sense of well-being. Conscious evolution is like that. We need the willingness to abandon whatever no longer serves us—in both our outer and inner lives. When we do that we allow new life to emerge.

Chapter Twelve

NOW WHAT?

"Thoroughly unprepared, we take the step into the afternoon of life. Worse still, we take this step with the false presupposition that our truths and our ideals will serve us as hitherto. But we cannot live the afternoon of life according to the program of life's morning, for what was great in the morning will be little at evening and what in the morning was true, at evening will have become a lie."

—Carl Jung

Courage to Change

It requires courage to unlearn and relinquish the ideas and truths that were once useful to us but now hold us back. It also requires the certainty that we are not our ideas or beliefs. All the world's conflict and strife—both personal and global—is caused by differences of opinion. Every war that was ever fought was based on differing points of view. Added to that was the unwillingness of either side to allow the other side to have *its* point of view.

Living in the Question

I like to say that *"Ego seeks answers, Spirit asks questions."* A shift happens when we release the need to find definitive answers to our questions about life and the world around us. Have you ever noticed that the primary function of the mind seems to be finding answers? We are trained from a young age that there is a right answer to every question. Our entire educational system is based on memorizing information and being able to regurgitate the answers come test time. In one reality, there is a correct answer to some of life's questions. However, even in that version of reality, those answers sometimes change based on new information or new ways of seeing the situation. I am reminded of how much our "factual" world has changed over time. Science is continuously revealing how things are not as solid as we once believed.

How willing are we to live *with*, and *in* questions, recognizing them as potentially more important than the answers? When we grasp too tightly onto answers, it shuts down our process of inquiry and puts limits on our capacity to understand. Willingness to live in a question opens us up to deeper and greater knowing. It opens us up to infinite possibilities rather than staying stuck in our normal way of seeing things. It allows us to expand beyond our previous limits of comprehension. When we live within a question, we dig deeper into our internal exploration of what's possible, rather than reaching for an answer that is already known. Living in the question invites us to travel into mystery. Spirit loves the unknown. It loves mystery. The mind is constantly seeking answers. That's its function. However, the answers it comes up with keep us separate from the truth of who we *really* are.

Concepts and Ideologies

When we "collapse in" on an idea, we create our life in that way. This is now being proven by the field of quantum physics. There are infinite possibilities in any situation. When we focus on one, it comes into manifestation. So, what I'm suggesting is to look at the question: "What else is possible?" It's not about what we collapse in on, but what we expand upon which matters. Can we open up to even more possibility? Can we loosen the grip of our ego? Can we let go of and recognize that our stories around it are limited based on our experiences, perceptions, and point of view?

When our conscious awareness changes—and we move beyond choosing, beyond limitation—we actually enter into a new way of being. And that new way of being is free from clinging to concepts. When we live in that space, everything changes. The Course in Miracles states: *"The greatest tool for changing the world is to change our mind about the world."* I'll take that one step further by saying the greatest way we can change the world is to detach from *all* of the concepts we hold to be true. That includes theologies and ideologies. Everything changes when we tap into that deepest, truest part of our self. And it's not really even a part—it actually is the truth of who we are.

Spiritual Inquiry

It is not helpful to tell our minds to stop seeking answers. That would be like telling our heart to stop pumping blood or our lungs to stop breathing. But we can lessen the importance we give to those answers. That is primarily because the answers our minds come up with are always based in our level of consciousness. In other words, nothing changes if nothing changes. If we are always listening to and being guided only by our mind's answers, nothing can ever change in our life. We are reminded that all we know is not all there is to know. The practice of living in the question is actually quite simple. When we notice our minds collapsing in on an idea or an answer, we simply pause and ask ourselves a question or a series of questions.

A common method for practicing spiritual inquiry is to repeat a chosen question, over and over again. With each repetition, the mind is given the opportunity to stretch a little further, and then a little further, as it seeks an answer. Expanding the mind's capacity to know, in this way, takes us into new dimensions of understanding. Using this method, the question itself is more important than the answer. After some time of doing this, you may notice that the "answers" seem to come from a deeper place than the mind. That is when it can get really interesting. This inquiry process can either be done alone or with a partner. If done with a partner, start by sitting and facing each other. Person A asks person B the question, and listens for an answer. Person B gives a short answer. Without responding, person A then repeats the same question, and so on, for whatever period of time you choose. I recommend asking the question repeatedly for at least three minutes.

What Is The Valuable Question?

Here is a list of questions designed to open you to infinite possibilities rather than collapsing in on finite answers. You may try these questions, or create your own. Notice the questions are open-ended. That means they cannot be answered with a yes or no. And they do not start with "Why...?" It has been said that "why" is not a spiritual question. That's because the mind believes answering "why" will "fix" you or a situation. And remember, you are not broken.

Who are you?

What are you?

What is love?

What is spirit?

What is ego?

What is pain?

What is heaven?

What is hell?

How does life get even better than this?

What else is possible?

Here's the great news…we don't know what else is possible, in our minds. But we do know infinite possibility in our being. When we live in the question, we access a deeper understanding and a deeper knowing, and we also open ourselves up to more and more possibilities in our lives.

The Opinion Trap

Our egos love opinions and the feeling of superiority we get from sharing those opinions with anyone who will listen. Some years ago, I took the "spiritual challenge" of going 30 days without an opinion. I started by simply agreeing not to *voice* my opinions, but I quickly recognized I was only keeping them trapped inside. My mind was racing with thoughts, opinions, and perspectives. Only when I *actually* loosened the grip of opinions did I feel the benefit of this process. After some time, I began to notice when practicing this, I felt closer and more connected to the people around me. I felt a presence and a spaciousness that was liberating in many ways. I felt more love flowing out of me. I was actually *available* to the present moment and to the people and situations in my life. It was, and continues to be, a life-changing practice.

Often, when I share this process, people respond with something like: *"Aren't we supposed to have opinions? Isn't that how we are designed?"* Perhaps that is true. But, if we are willing to look, we can plainly see how much negative energy is produced by people feeling the need to voice their opinions. And the result is almost always separation. We now have entire websites and businesses dedicated to gathering and sharing opinions. Watch most any TV news program today, and you will see heated arguments from two different "sides" or opinions on a particular topic. In the end, my question is: "Is this 'opinion giving' culture bringing us closer together, or moving us farther apart?" Are we experiencing more love, more joy, and more harmony? The answer seems almost too obvious to answer.

Not Knowing

The Zen concept of "beginners mind" speaks to the willingness to *not know*. Remaining open to life, without needing to have answers, is an effective way of stepping outside the confines of our thinking minds. We can experience the state of wonder and innocence that is characteristic of living at the mystical level of awareness. When we live from this place, we realize that our ideas and opinions are just that. It is tremendously liberating when we shift from *needing to know*, to the freedom of *being curious*. When we are able to relax into *not knowing*, we experience true safety. We are no longer under the control or dictates of the mind. When we are no longer controlled by the mind, we are free of its limits. We can experience the unbounded realm where infinite peace and love are *always present*. As long as we remain identified *with* and trapped *in* our thinking minds, the unbounded, infinite realm remains out of our reach. The thinking mind is not capable of experiencing the unlimited. The unlimited is beyond all thought. To take this a step further, if we wish to know ourselves *as* the infinite, we may even choose to not only go beyond answers, but even beyond asking questions.

The Hundredth Monkey

The term "hundredth monkey effect" was coined in the late 1950s when a group of scientists were studying the behavior of the snow monkey (Japanese macaque), on an island in Japan. The scientists threw sweet potatoes to the monkeys, and the potatoes landed in the sand. Although the monkeys liked eating the potatoes, they didn't like the sand that stuck to them. One day, a monkey was observed taking her potato to water and washing the sand off before eating it. She taught this method to her family members and over a period of a few years, most of the monkeys on the island learned to wash their potatoes. Around this time, the scientists were surprised to observe that monkeys on nearby islands were also washing their potatoes before eating them—even though they had not been taught to do so. The scientists deduced that when a certain critical mass of individual monkeys had learned the new behavior, a tipping point was reached. The new knowledge was transferred, through collective consciousness, to the whole population of monkeys. The hypothetical "100th monkey" tipped the balance.

Many people believe that when a critical mass of human beings has shifted into the new consciousness, the whole human race will automatically shift. Before a tipping point is reached, the new consciousness remains the assets of the individuals who have shifted. However, when the critical mass is reached, the new consciousness will spread throughout humanity, becoming the shared perspective of all. The personal transformational work that each individual does for themselves is therefore the *most* important contribution to the whole of humanity.

One Life

As we do the work of clearing our vision, we come to realize that goodness is everywhere. We were just unable to see it before cleaning the lens through which we see life. We discover that the same goodness we find at the core of ourselves is at the core of every other human. It is at the core of all existence. This inherent essence of love is the level at which we are all one. Oneness means that there is only one life. Everything emerges from one source. We are all unique expressions of that one life. Nothing can possibly exist outside of it. There is a story about a young avatar, living in a village, who was known as a healer and a mystic. Villagers would come from far and wide to seek answers from the boy. One inquirer said: "I'll give you an orange if you tell me where God is." The avatar responded: "I'll give you two if you can tell me where God isn't."

The New Meditation

Welcome to the new paradigm. This is a new way of being in the world. We are not, in the 21st century, looking for a messiah or prophet to come. We are not looking to follow prescribed doctrines or rigid ideologies. We are now ready to listen to the evolutionary impulse that is propelling us forward *from within* into this new era. We are now ready to be guided by the divine intelligence of our being. What was once for a select few—Buddha, Jesus, Lao Tsu—is now a way of being for us all.

It is now time for each of us to take our meditation practice with us wherever we go. My invitation for you is to move from your meditation pillows and take to the streets *being* meditation. This is how we change the world; this is how we serve the new paradigm. We are here to *be* presence, *be* love, and *be* peace in the world. Our commitment to bringing present-moment awareness into the world is our highest calling.

A Greater Reality

This greater reality is based on nothing you have ever learned, yet everything you already know. My wish for you is that you fully awaken to the realization that you are *already one with the whole of existence*—whether you call that God, Goddess, Love, Light, Life, Source, Spirit, Universe, or by any other name. This fundamental understanding will permanently change your life. There is nothing you need to become. You already *are* everything you seek. All you need to do is remember your true identity, and have the courage to speak and act from that in the world.

A gentle reminder of the truth:
You are Peace
You are Love
You are Light
You are the one you have been waiting for.

You are here to awaken and open your
heart to a new way of being.
THE TIME IS NOW!

INDEX

A

Abundance 48, 109, 110, 111, 112, 113, 114, 115, 118

Acceptance xv, 10, 35, 52, 107, 118, 127

Action 7, 8, 23, 31, 35, 36, 51, 53, 58, 66, 84, 85, 87, 88, 93, 105, 106, 114

Addiction 16, 17, 19, 31, 32, 33, 45, 47, 71, 81, 119, 122, 124, 125

Affirmations 20, 47, 48, 54

Attachment 48, 78, 116, 123, 127, 133

Awakened Living 1, 9, 10, 12, 13, 19, 40, 69, 83

Awakening xvi, 1, 2, 12, 13, 39, 57, 74, 75, 78, 79, 105, 111, 114, 129, 137, 139

Awareness 2, 4, 5, 11, 12, 27, 35, 36, 38, 39, 44, 46, 47, 48, 52, 53, 54, 55, 56, 58, 74, 77, 84, 85, 97, 102, 104, 105, 110, 112, 122, 125, 132, 133, 137, 140, 143, 146, 149

B

Beginners Mind 146

Being xvi, 1, 2, 7, 8, 10, 12, 15, 16, 19, 22, 24, 25, 26, 30, 32, 33, 34, 36, 39, 40, 44, 45, 46, 49, 50, 55, 56, 57, 60, 61, 62, 63, 64, 65, 66, 68, 70, 71, 74, 75, 79, 82, 83, 84, 85, 87, 88, 89, 94, 95, 97, 103, 104, 105, 106, 110, 115, 117, 120, 121, 124, 125, 126, 128, 132, 133, 135, 137, 139, 140, 142, 143, 144, 145, 146, 147, 148, 149

Blessings 67, 77

Buddha 149

Buddhism 131, 133

C

Change 5, 7, 8, 12, 13, 18, 19, 21, 23, 26, 27, 44, 46, 47, 48, 58, 60, 61, 62, 66, 67, 68, 73, 75, 79, 82, 85, 86, 101, 104, 105, 107, 109, 110, 112, 120, 121, 128, 129, 131, 132, 133, 134, 135, 139, 141, 142, 143, 144, 149

Compassion 11, 15, 17, 18, 24, 35, 37, 53, 66, 72, 85, 100, 103, 104, 107, 120

Competition 57, 138, 139

Concepts xvi, 1, 2, 3, 7, 26, 31, 36, 48, 60, 78, 83, 98, 110, 112, 138, 143, 146

Consciousness 2, 3, 4, 5, 9, 11, 12,
        13, 21, 22, 27, 32, 36, 37, 38,
        39, 43, 44, 45, 46, 47, 48, 49,
        51, 53, 54, 55, 56, 57, 58, 60,
        61, 62, 63, 64, 65, 66, 67, 72,
        80, 82, 84, 85, 90, 105, 107,
        114, 115, 120, 128, 129, 133,
        137, 138, 139, 143, 147, 148
Cooperation 138, 139

D

Death 75, 76, 80, 81, 82, 83,
        119, 126
Denial 19, 23, 127
Disorientation 68
Divine 13, 41, 49, 51, 54, 62, 110,
        115, 117, 136, 137, 148
Doing 8, 10, 16, 20, 21, 24, 45, 50,
        51, 66, 74, 83, 84, 87, 88, 91,
        92, 94, 95, 101, 110, 113, 116,
        122, 126, 135, 144

E

Ego 6, 16, 22, 29, 37, 48, 49, 68, 71,
        74, 75, 76, 83, 101, 107, 114,
        119, 123, 124, 125, 127, 133,
        136, 142, 145
Energy 22, 48, 51, 55, 63, 75, 92, 93,
        95, 101, 103, 110, 119, 126,
        134, 146
Enlightenment 1, 2, 6, 39, 66, 137
Evolution 4, 43, 58, 62, 68, 110, 140

F

Fear 2, 5, 6, 31, 33, 34, 35, 45, 50,
        63, 64, 65, 70, 80, 82, 91, 94,
        97, 98, 99, 103, 104, 120,
        124, 125, 127, 133
Forgiveness 36, 104, 109, 110

Freedom xv, 2, 9, 32, 38, 41, 56, 69,
        70, 71, 76, 78, 109, 116, 146

G

God 2, 8, 13, 22, 23, 30, 44, 45, 51,
        53, 54, 55, 61, 62, 71, 103,
        110, 113, 124, 148, 149
God Mind 54, 61, 110
Gratitude xv, xvii, 21, 22, 70, 82,
        111, 121
Guilt 114, 135

H

Happiness 21, 23, 24, 26, 44, 48,
        50, 58, 113, 115, 127
Heart xvii, 8, 15, 16, 30, 50, 52, 54,
        60, 61, 65, 66, 67, 69, 75, 81,
        89, 90, 91, 93, 95, 98, 127,
        134, 137, 143, 149
Heaven 26, 27, 59, 60, 64, 68, 69,
        70, 71, 72, 145
Hell 27, 59, 60, 64, 65, 145
Honesty 34

I

Ideologies 143, 148
Illusion 6, 39, 40, 41, 65, 66, 68,
        70, 73, 74, 100, 105, 110,
        115, 136
Impermanence 23, 132
Inquiry 56, 114, 139, 142, 143, 144
Integration 35, 117, 118
Intuition 50, 58, 65, 69, 90, 93, 95

J

Jesus 27, 126, 149
Judgment 6, 11, 18, 24, 26, 70, 76,
        81, 100, 110, 112, 117, 134

K

Karma 7, 74
Knowing xv, 1, 3, 10, 13, 16, 20, 48,
 50, 55, 60, 65, 66, 67, 69, 78,
 82, 83, 85, 88, 90, 91, 92, 97,
 100, 101, 103, 105, 106, 110,
 113, 118, 121, 122, 128, 132,
 134, 142, 145, 146

L

Lao Tsu vii, 149
Law of Attraction 113
Light xv, 4, 7, 8, 9, 10, 13, 20, 27,
 35, 40, 55, 66, 69, 75, 78,
 101, 102, 110, 111, 119, 123,
 137, 149
Limitation 19, 37, 38, 39, 40,
 137, 143
Living in the Question 142, 144
Love xvi, xvii, 3, 8, 9, 10, 13, 15, 17,
 18, 20, 22, 25, 35, 37, 40, 45,
 48, 50, 51, 52, 54, 55, 58, 66,
 67, 69, 70, 80, 85, 90, 97, 98,
 99, 100, 102, 103, 104, 105,
 106, 107, 110, 111, 120, 123,
 124, 125, 135, 137, 142, 145,
 146, 148, 149

M

Magical 44, 47, 48, 54, 57, 62, 94
Manifestation 115
Martyr 43, 44, 45, 46, 49, 53, 57, 62
Meditation 55, 56, 81, 89, 101, 102,
 110, 114, 148, 149
Metaphysical 23, 37, 44, 48, 49, 50,
 51, 54, 63
Mind 1, 3, 4, 6, 8, 18, 23, 25, 30, 31,
 39, 40, 43, 48, 49, 50, 52, 54,
 56, 58, 59, 60, 61, 62, 64, 65,
 66, 67, 69, 74, 76, 77, 82, 88,
 89, 90, 91, 92, 93, 95, 100,
 101, 102, 103, 105, 106, 109,
 110, 113, 118, 121, 127, 131,
 134, 137, 138, 142, 143, 144,
 145, 146, 147
Mystical xvi, xvii, 21, 23, 44, 51, 52,
 54, 103, 104, 105, 107, 146

N

New Age 7, 54
New Thought 7, 47, 54, 61, 62, 63,
 126, 128

O

Oneness xv, 4, 6, 8, 10, 20, 24, 54,
 59, 61, 64, 65, 66, 69, 79, 85,
 90, 95, 107, 113, 115, 118,
 128, 137, 148
Opinions 10, 67, 76, 78, 141,
 145, 146

P

Pain 18, 34, 46, 47, 63, 67, 77, 109,
 119, 126, 127, 133, 134, 145
Paradigm 20, 44, 45, 58, 60, 61, 62,
 104, 114, 119, 120, 121, 132,
 137, 138, 148, 149
Peace xvi, 2, 10, 23, 33, 52, 54, 58,
 59, 65, 66, 69, 70, 75, 79, 85,
 90, 95, 103, 109, 110, 112,
 127, 146, 149
Perfection 19, 20, 40, 54, 95, 97,
 100, 115, 118
Perspective xvi, 6, 8, 12, 20, 21, 23,
 24, 30, 31, 49, 52, 55, 57, 66,
 67, 69, 76, 80, 82, 90, 95, 104,
 112, 120, 135, 139, 145
Prayer 21, 55

Prosperity 113
Purpose xv, 10, 40, 49, 50, 51, 67,
    77, 78, 84, 87, 88, 89, 91, 92,
    93, 94, 110, 114, 115, 119,
    122, 123, 127, 128, 134

Q

Quantum Physics 48, 78, 137
Questions xv, 3, 30, 38, 43, 46, 52,
    55, 65, 78, 88, 91, 93, 99, 105,
    112, 113, 122, 136, 137, 142,
    144, 145, 146, 147

R

Reality xv, xvi, 4, 6, 7, 8, 9, 12, 29,
    31, 39, 40, 44, 46, 47, 48, 49,
    50, 51, 54, 55, 56, 60, 64, 66,
    70, 72, 73, 74, 76, 77, 79, 99,
    104, 105, 117, 128, 137, 138,
    139, 140, 142, 149
Realization 1, 3, 4, 9, 105, 125, 149
Rebirth 80, 83
Recovery 16, 19, 95, 122
Religion 1, 13, 26, 45, 54, 58, 61,
    129, 139
Resistance 10, 18, 23, 57, 83, 94,
    100, 101, 110, 112, 131
Right 2, 3, 6, 10, 11, 15, 21, 23, 26,
    30, 35, 44, 45, 48, 50, 51, 52,
    64, 69, 70, 72, 73, 76, 77, 84,
    94, 95, 98, 109, 110, 111, 112,
    113, 117, 123, 139, 142
Romantic Love 98

S

Security 5, 116, 117, 131
Self-Love 50, 106, 107
Self-Realization 1, 3, 9, 125
Separateness 6, 65, 90

Shadow 10, 20, 33, 34, 35, 100
Shame xv, 114, 135
Silence 89, 101, 110
Soul 74, 115, 126
Source 13, 20, 22, 24, 49, 50, 51, 52,
    60, 61, 63, 65, 66, 69, 70, 89,
    90, 99, 102, 107, 112, 113,
    115, 117, 121, 128, 136, 138,
    148, 149
Spirit 16, 41, 51, 55, 71, 74, 88, 89,
    91, 118, 123, 124, 127, 132,
    133, 142, 145, 149
Spiritual xv, xvi, xvii, 1, 2, 12, 15,
    17, 18, 19, 20, 24, 26, 31, 32,
    33, 35, 36, 38, 40, 46, 47, 55,
    56, 57, 58, 60, 61, 62, 63, 64,
    65, 70, 71, 72, 74, 75, 78, 79,
    81, 82, 83, 85, 86, 91, 92, 93,
    101, 102, 105, 111, 112, 113,
    114, 115, 117, 119, 122, 123,
    124, 125, 127, 135, 139, 143,
    144, 145
Spiritual Bypass 36
Spiritual Teachers xvii, 1, 15, 20,
    70, 71, 83, 91
Spiritual Truth xvi, 64
Suffering 16, 26, 56, 65, 77, 84, 98,
    106, 126, 127, 131, 133, 134
Support xvii, 8, 11, 12, 37, 40, 57,
    67, 70, 78, 79, 84, 85, 92, 93,
    94, 101, 102, 114
Surrender 7, 13, 22, 41, 49, 55, 62,
    71, 127

T

The Great Remembering 100
Transformation 12, 35, 60, 61, 66,
    68, 77, 78, 80, 83, 93, 94, 125
True Nature xv, 2, 3, 4, 8, 9, 35, 59,
    71, 103, 106

U

Ultimate Reality 40, 74
Unity 56, 62
Unlearning 3, 29, 31

V

Victim 9, 44, 45, 46, 53, 62, 63,
      80, 84
Vision 24, 95, 104, 105, 135, 148

W

Wholeness 2, 19, 20, 21, 29, 30, 32,
      33, 34, 40, 41, 79, 97, 99, 100,
      121, 125, 127
Wisdom 17, 66, 91, 93
Witness Consciousness 5, 9, 11

Made in the USA
San Bernardino, CA
01 October 2016